DRUIDCRAFT

DRUIDCRAFT

The Magic of
Wicca & Druidry

Philip Carr-Gomm

Thorsons

Thorsons
An Imprint of HarperCollins*Publishers*
77–85 Fulham Palace Road
Hammersmith, London W6 8JB

The Thorsons website address is:
www.thorsons.com

and Thorsons
are trademarks of
HarperCollins*Publishers* Limited

Published by Thorsons 2002

1 3 5 7 9 10 8 6 4 2

© Philip Carr-Gomm 2002

Philip Carr-Gomm asserts the moral right to be
identified as the author of this work

A catalogue record for this book
is available from the British Library

ISBN 0 00 713388 X

Illustrations by Chris Down

Printed and bound in Great Britain by
Creative Print and Design, Wales (Ebbw Vale)

Dedication

To Stephanie, my muse and my love, who has offered the inspiration
for so many of the ideas given here and in my other books

Contents

Acknowledgements

For years I have wanted to write this book – the subject of the relationship between Wicca and Druidry has intrigued me from the moment I began to study Druidry over 30 years ago with my teacher, Ross Nichols. I would like to thank Ross for all the encouragement he gave his young student – I had no idea at the time how important his encouragement would be, and how much it would mean to me today.

My wife Stephanie's constant encouragement and her perceptive insights throughout the writing of this book have also proved invaluable and are deeply appreciated.

I would also like to thank Susan Henssler, who commented in detail on the draft manuscript, and whose inspired wording I have used for much of the ritual passages. My deep gratitude also goes to Ronald Hutton who, with great attention and characteristic enthusiasm, commented in depth on the manuscript. His eye for detail and his considerable knowledge of the history of Witchcraft and Wicca gave me the confidence to tread in this barely charted territory. My thanks go to Ellen Evert Hopman who inspired me with her account of a candle-boat ceremony, and who helped me track down elusive information, and also to Carole Nielsen for her herbal wisom, and to Erynn Laurie for her elucidation of the Irish versions of the term 'Druidcraft'. My thanks also go to Cairisthea Worthington for inspiring me with her vision of the four faces of the Goddess, and to Vivianne Crowley for her contribution to this book and for the inspiration I have gained from her writing. And a big thank you to Matthew Cory, editor of this book, for his sensitivity and persistence in dealing with such a stubborn author.

Finally, I would like to acknowledge the inspiration I have gained from the camps held by The Order of Bards Ovates and Druids in the vale of the White Horse over the last eight years. There we have explored the practice of a new kind of 'Wild Druidry' – a 'Druidcraft' that is earthy and spirited in a way that allows us to go beyond the labels of 'Druid', 'Wiccan'or 'Pagan', bringing us closer to the Way which is Nameless, the Old Way which is ever new and ever-changing.

Foreword

Philip's beautiful and eloquent book is a new but ancient vision that will be a source of inspiration to Druids, Wiccans and all those drawn to nature spirituality and magic. In *Druidcraft* we see Druidry restoring its persecuted and suppressed tradition of magic and seership and moving closer to Wicca. The gap is increasingly small, as both traditions seek to reawaken contemporary culture to what we might call 'natural religion', our instinctive reaching out to venerate the planet that is our home, to celebrate the Divine within one another and within all creation, and to honour the ever-changing seasons and cycles of nature and human life.

Druidry and Wicca share a love and veneration for the natural world and have an important role to play in restoring aspects of spiritual tradition too long neglected, to our own cost. This includes the vision of the Divine as immanent and present all around us in the glorious wonder of the natural world of our own planet and that of the cosmos. It includes too the vision of the Divine not as God, but as Goddess and God. These images of the Divine interconnect in mutual harmony to create an interchange of energies that gives birth to new life; for the sum of the whole is truly greater than that of the parts. *Druidcraft* reflects this synthesis, integrating in a refreshingly new and unique way nature spirituality and magical vision, veneration for the Divine as Goddess and God, and the integration of body and spirit – engagement with and joy in this world, as well as the journey to unification with Ultimate Reality that is at the heart of human existence.

My own path is Wicca, but Druidry also had a strong attraction. I visited Ross Nichols, Philip's predecessor as Chosen Chief of the Order of Bards, Ovates and Druids, thirty years ago. A wise and kindly man, he took time in his busy schedule to explain Druidry to a teenage spiritual seeker trying to find the right path. Druidry offered much, but the Goddess orientation, greater female leadership, and the focus on the development of those powers of the human psyche that we call magic in Wicca proved the stronger pull. Since then, much has changed. Druidry has developed greater interest in the traditional magical skills and gifts of its Druid ancestors, and the role of women in Druidry now equals that of men. Wicca has grown closer to Druidry in its provision for family participation and openness as a path for the many rather than the few. Both traditions have evolved to see themselves as part of a growing contemporary spirituality that is concerned with social engagement, planetary responsibility, and providing meaningful philosophy and ethics by which people may live in our increasingly complex multi-cultural world.

Druidcraft reflects a growing trend in contemporary Paganism, a strengthening of each of the Pagan traditions as they learn from one another, and the cross-fertilization that is the fruit of those who have explored both traditions to draw them together in their own unique synthesis.

Vivianne Crowley

Chapter One

A Hidden Valley

The Worlds of the Witch & Druid

Earth and Her stones, shining stars of the night sky,
tumbling rivers, cauldrons, magic, ancient wisdom, strange
hidden beauty, inner knowing, seeing beyond the veil of
Time, knowing that I will return again to Earth after death,
loving my fellow humans, my body and all animals, flying
like a bird to the sun, like a bat to the moon, kissing the
standing stone, drinking from the grail.

Oh that I could see to the Other Realm -
that I could learn the magic of the Ancients.
Oh that the secrets of the Druids and the Witches
could be whispered in my ears
that I might know their beauty and their power -
that I might love again this land
and hear the voices of the Goddess and the God
in the trees and in the rivers.

If you ever travel to Avalon in the south-west of England, you will find, tucked between the crouching beast that is Glastonbury Tor and the rounded breast that is Chalice Hill, a magical garden surrounding a well steeped in legend. Here, between the two hills – one so strongly 'masculine' and the other so clearly 'feminine' – the well and its garden exude an extraordinary sense of peace and deep resonant power. If you were to enter that garden now you would pass lawns and flower beds, low hedgerows and gnarled yew trees until, following the path that slopes gently upward, you would arrive at the wellhead. And there you would find the well itself, protected by a finely wrought iron cover depicting an ancient symbol – the *vesica piscis*.

In this symbol, two circles overlap and in doing so create an image which for some depicts Christ, for others the philosopher's stone, and for yet others the Holy Grail or the sacred vulva of the Goddess. The symbol depicts the union of two principles, two beings, two powers. Each circle remains intact, complete and whole, but where they meet something different and unique is created from their union.

This book takes two worlds which are complete and whole in themselves, and brings them together. It is at the point where they meet that we can, if we wish, find a path of great depth and power.

The worlds that are brought together in this book are those of Witchcraft and Druidry, and I have called the path that they create together Druidcraft, from the Irish word Druidecht, and from the inspiration of the Irish poet W.B. Yeats who uses this term in his poetry.

Many people now practise either Druidry (also known as Druidism) or Wicca (as Witchcraft is often called today) and find within their paths all that they need. Each tradition is complete in itself, and I am not suggesting that either way is incomplete or inadequate. However, over the years I have noticed that many Wiccans have become interested in Druidry, just as many Druids have become interested in Wicca. The fact is that the two circles of Druidry and Wicca now overlap, as many people start to combine their knowledge and experience of each path to fashion their own 'craft' – their own spiritual way. For these people the synthesis explored in this book is already happening.

Some time ago there was a real difference between the concerns of Wiccans and Druids. Wiccans were interested in magic and spells, while Druids were more interested in history, the old Celtic myths and a 'spiritual' rather than 'magical' approach to life. But in the last few years this has changed. Many Wiccans have become interested in the history of the Druids, in Celtic myths, and in Druid animal and tree lore. At the same time, many Druids have become interested in the more intuitive and magical approaches to life that are found in Wicca. If you talk to people who are interested in Wicca or Druidry you will find that most of them are drawn to these spiritual paths for the same reasons.

In the past, subjects and disciplines were kept within defined boundaries. Today, we understand the value of synthesis, synergy and interdisciplinary studies. This is the spirit in which this book is written – to contribute to the field, not to detract from the uniqueness of each approach. I respect both paths deeply and I believe that each is complete in itself, but this does not mean that their relationship and connections cannot be explored, and we may even discover that

Wicca and Druidry have gifts to offer that we can combine in creative and beneficial ways.

Most people think that Druidry and Wicca, as they are practised today, represent two streams of pagan tradition that have evolved separately over centuries, or even millennia. In reality, the modern versions of these traditions were originally developed by two friends, Ross Nichols and Gerald Gardner, only 50 years ago. Because of their exchange of ideas and knowledge, the two paths share many similarities and points of connection and, to a great extent, the differences between them are related to the differences between their characters, even though over the last half-century both paths have evolved considerably, creating many different varieties and styles of both Wiccan and Druidic practice.

Druidry and Wicca are now strong and vibrant spiritualities, and if either of them provides you with all that you need, no further exploration is necessary. But if, like me, you can't resist the urge to explore a hidden valley where two lands meet, then however great the risks, you might well choose to put on your hiking boots, throw a pack on your back and set off!

Loaded Words and Dangerous Cults

The words Witch and Druid evoke a longing in many of us for the wisdom of the past and of the ancestors. They evoke images of mystery and magic, of ancient knowledge of the Earth and her seasons, of star-lore and herb-lore, of primal wisdom and inner knowing. But they are words that can also evoke anxiety. Some people believe that Witches and Druids are members of dangerous cults, and even though we may know that this is nonsense, there is no point in pretending that the words 'Witch' and 'Druid' are not loaded. Some people think at once of sorcery and Satanism – they see the Witches of Shakespeare's *Macbeth* tossing bats' wings into bubbling cauldrons, and Druid priests raising gleaming blades above the bodies of virgins sprawled across the 'Slaughter Stone' at Stonehenge.

These negative images of Witchcraft and Druidry come mostly from the scaremongering of fundamentalist Christian groups and from the tacky products of the movie and publishing industries. The genre of the horror movie needs constant feeding, and Shakespeare, together with later writers about 'spooky Witchcraft', have provided them with ample material.

It is true that Roman writers talked of Druids being present at human sacrifices, but we need to put this in context: Christian priests are present at executions today, and in ancient times human sacrifice was a feature of many societies. The Romans themselves sacrificed people until the first century BC. After that, they secularized the activity, built the Colosseum, and turned death into public entertainment.

It is also true that during the witch-hunts of the fifteenth, sixteenth and seventeenth centuries, people confessed to being Witches, cursing others and having sexual intercourse with the Devil. But only the most obtuse people fail to see a connection between these confessions and the fact that they were extracted by torture.

Every religion or spiritual path has its share of insane and unpleasant people, and there are likely to have been some malevolent Druids and Witches, just as there have been malevolent Christians. But with the Inquisition and the Crusades, a body count would undoubtedly stack up unfavourably towards the latter.

Another misconception is that Druids and Witches practise Satanism. To do this you must believe in a being called Satan, and to practise it involves performing a reverse Christian ritual known as a Black Mass. Druids and Witches do not believe in an entity called Satan, or one who acts in the way he is supposed to act. They certainly do not per-form reverse Christian ceremonies of any kind. In fact, some Druids are Christian and for several years I have attended conferences on Druidry and Christianity held at an abbey in Gloucestershire, England. There have also been conferences where Witches, Christians and Druids have shared their ideas in a spirit of tolerance and under-standing. The two seminal thinkers who developed Druidry and Witchcraft in the modern era, Nichols and Gardner, were both ordained Christians. So, if you want to be spooked, you need to look elsewhere!

The World of the Wise Folk

Wiccans call their tradition 'The Craft of the Wise', and the historic figures with whom many people identify most strongly are those in a community who were called upon to offer cures, help deliver babies and assist those dying, find people or objects with psychic sight, and to help in times of individual or communal difficulty. Your spouse is sleeping with another person; there has been no rain on your land for months; your cattle are dying from a mysterious disease; your best knife has been stolen; your baby's cough will not go away; you know you are dying and are frightened – all these are problems that needed to be faced in the past, just as they need to be faced today. Nowadays we turn to scientists, counsellors, doctors, vets, police officers and priests. In the old days, we went to those men and women who knew about the mysteries of life, who were called to heal and to help. Through their own experience, through communion with spirits and teachers from the Otherworld, and through training from those who had been drawn to the Ways before them, they would each come to be known and respected as the local wise woman or man of their community. In parts of Britain they were known as Cunning Men and Women, from the root word 'con' or 'ken', which means 'to know'. They were the wise ones, the people with 'Knowledge'.

Historians now believe that it is unlikely that these people ever met together in 'covens' to work magic in the way that witch finders and modern writers have described. Instead, it seems far more likely that they worked as the local wise person, using their knowledge of spellcraft, herbalism and natural magic to help the local community in the ways described. It is also likely that they trained one or two other people in their craft, often from within their own family. Clearly, the Cunning Folk were in positions of great influence within their community. They seemed to possess the power of life and death, and of secret knowledge, and if they failed to save a life or if a villager grew worse under their care, one can imagine the hatred this might have provoked. Powerful people evoke respect and admiration, but they can soon be turned upon with a fury that matches in intensity the awe in which they are held. To become a Cunning person required devotion and courage, as well as both practical and psychic skills. As with all professions that require the use of power, there are always unscrupulous practitioners who will prey on the gullibility and superstitions of others, and who will do anything for money or favours, hence the fear of 'wicked Witches', 'evil magicians' – people who will, for a price, use their abilities not to heal but to harm.

The World of the Druid

While the Cunning Folk worked alone or in small groups, and were the local wise people and healers in rural communities, the Druids were an organized elite, exempt from warfare and paying taxes, and they acted as judges, teachers, philosophers and advisers to chieftains, kings and queens. They appear very different to the image that we hold of Witches, until we examine them in more detail.

The origins of Druidism are lost in the mists of time. All we can say is that gradually, as successive migrations of peoples from as far away as Anatolia and Caucasia arrived in Ireland and the British Isles, their spiritual beliefs and magical practices mingled with those of the indigenous population, and at a certain time these became focused within the great stone circles. Later, as more migrations occurred, tribes which have come to be labelled as Celtic settled in these lands, and Druidism evolved as both a spiritual and cultural force that existed from Ireland in the West to Brittany in the East, and possibly as far as Anatolia, now Turkey. Druidism flourished for over a thousand years until the arrival of Christianity. By the sixth century it had ceased to exist in its complete form, and it was only revived after another thousand years, in the seventeenth century.

During the time that Druidry flourished, the classical writers tell us that they were organized into three groupings – Bards, Ovates and Druids. The Druids were teachers and philosophers; the Bards were poets, storytellers and musicians, who used their knowledge of the power of the word and of sound to inspire and enthral, to entertain and to charm – and even to bewitch.

The Ovates were seers and diviners, and it seems likely that they were also healers, herbalists and midwives. They have been variously termed by classical writers as *Vates, Uatis, Euhages*, and the word 'ovate' may derive from the Indo-European root *uat*, 'to be inspired or possessed'. The classical author Strabo described the Ovate as 'an interpreter of nature'. It was the Ovates who were skilled in reading omens and divining auguries – whether from the flight of birds, the shape of clouds, or the behaviour of animals or the weather – and it was the Ovates whose task it was to heal, using their knowledge of herbs and spells to cure disease in humans and livestock. The Ovate seems, in numerous ways, identical to the type of person many people would describe as a Witch. But what became of the Ovates?

With the triumph of Christianity over all indigenous faiths in Britain by about the sixth century, the Bardic tradition continued, with schools of Bards existing in Ireland, Wales and Scotland until the seventeenth century. The Druids, being the professional elite, were absorbed into the new dispensation. Nothing more is heard of the Ovates, who seem to simply disappear. Or did they? If you knew how to cure someone, would you stop doing this under a new religious order? Would you refrain from passing on your knowledge to your children, or to your students, so that they too might cure others? The same goes for midwifery skills, for the knowledge of tree, herb and animal lore, and for the ability to do magic, to make spells and potions. It is likely that, with the coming of Christianity, the Ovate stream of Druidry went underground but did not die out: you cannot prevent this kind of knowledge from being passed on – even though it may change in the passing.

It is possible that through word-of-mouth tradition, the Ovate stream of Druidry became one of the sources that fed later generations of healers and followers of the Old Ways, until they came to be known as the Cunning Folk. And it is primarily these Cunning people who are now held as Witches in modern popular perception.

Those who study Druidry today find that as they enter the Ovate period of their studies, they seem to develop and get in touch with precisely those parts of themselves that are now associated with the Witch, and that others associate with the shaman, including the ability to navigate the inner world, and develop seership.

When the two worlds of Witchcraft and Druidry are brought together, we find at the place of their meeting the figure of the Ovate-Witch who presides over a knowledge of the mysteries of Life and Death, whose cauldron offers the wisdom that is known in Druidry as Bright Knowledge.

Ovate and Witch

The words of the Bard lead us into the inner world, the Otherworld, that territory which lies beyond death, and that we visit sometimes in our dreams and our meditations. And even though the images, sounds and ideas that we experience there may seem less substantial than the 'reality' of our physical world, they often bring us inspiration and provide us with the guiding ideas and feelings that help us live out our lives. Once we learn how to tread the ways that lead into this Otherworld, we find ourselves in the realm of the Ovate-Witch – a realm presided over by the Goddess with her consort ever-present as the fertile God, Cernunnos as he is sometimes called. It is here that we learn of the mysteries of death and rebirth, and of the force that guides us through this process, the force of life itself – sexual energy. Imagine this force as a crystalline sparkling liquid in a cauldron of the Goddess, stirred by the God. As droplets fall from this cauldron, they bring energy and creative power to whoever and whatever they touch.

Change the image of the cauldron to that of a sacred well – a spring. The water in the well is this same energy, conveys the same power, and you see the water flowing from the sacred pool into a stream, which joins a river, which joins the sea. Water flows through the world, and through our bodies, and brings us life. And in death we are ferried across the waters to the Blessed Isles in the West, until after a time in the Summerlands, we are born again through the waters of the womb into new life on Earth.

This realm of water, of the cauldron, of life force, not only brings sensual pleasure and rebirth, but also healing and deep refreshment. If you gaze upon the surface of this sacred pool on the night of a full moon, you may be able to see beyond time, through time, to gain a deeper knowledge of your own being and of the fate of the world.

This is the realm of the Ovate, and I believe it is the realm of the Witch too. The outer forms of Ovate and Witch, or Druid and Wiccan practice may differ, but it is the same pool, the same wellspring that each hopes to contact. And the way that we can do this is through listening to the old stories, for that is the way, in an oral tradition, that spiritual teachings have always been conveyed.

The Forest School of Druidcraft

With the coming of Christianity to Ireland, many of the pagan ways were not lost – they simply took on a Christian gloss. Luckily, the old art of storytelling did not die. The new dispensation allowed the Bardic schools that were already established to continue taking pupils, and these flourished until the seventeenth century in Ireland, Wales and Scotland, retaining their memory of the old stories and their teachings of the creative power of music and voice.

So there you have the most amazing thing happening – the spiritual tradition of the Druids and Ovates as embodied in the Bards and their tales, is taught for over a thousand years, in modified and Christianized form in the Bardic schools. By the time the last of these schools closed its doors, the old tales were well and truly embedded in the collective mind – in folklore and in the popular imagination. The very landscape of Ireland and the British Isles is steeped in these tales, and all we need to do, to connect once again with their power and the teachings that they convey, is to journey into the land and listen to these old stories once again.

The tales then become our teacher, the wilderness and the forest our school.

An Invitation

Over the next five chapters you are invited to join just such a school, where we can listen to the songs of the Earth and the old tales, and explore that magical territory shared alike by Ovate and Witch, by Druidry and Wicca.

The Bard's Tale

Each chapter is like a lesson in this Forest School, and begins with a Bard telling a story, just as the teachers of the old Bardic schools told the old stories to generations of students, connecting those gathered around them to the current of ancestral wisdom that was conveyed in the vivid images and extraordinary events described.

In the stories that follow, I have retold some of these old Celtic tales – keeping to the structures and key themes of the old stories, but retelling them in my own way. These tales are meant to be told and retold in many different ways, and are not meant to be read as set in stone. Also, I deliberately refrain from explaining the stories too much. Their power lies in their ability to sneak past the rational mind and too much explanation destroys this power.

The Colloquy

Each tale is followed by a dialogue between a teacher and a pupil. The dialogue is a highly effective method of teaching – it was used in ancient Greece, and is well-known as the teaching method favoured by Socrates, in what has come to be known as the Socratic Dialogue. It was also used by the Druids and in Irish texts such a dialogue is known as a 'Colloquy', the most famous of which recounts the conversation between two poet-shamans in *The Colloquy of the Two Sages*.

Practical

After the Colloquy, the practical section of the lesson suggests ways in which you can work with the ideas presented. Just as the stories are not set in stone, neither are these. I see Druidcraft as a path of freedom and creativity. Both Wicca and Druidry offer tools, perspectives and sources of inspiration for us to craft our own practice. We can continue to honour tradition, while also honouring our own gifts and needs, making use of the materials and inspiration available, not only here, but also in the wonderfully varied worlds of Wicca, Druidry and allied subjects.

History

At the conclusion of each chapter, the history section answers the question: 'Where is all this coming from?' As you will see, the material presented is based on solid facts and historical sources. At the end of the book there is a Resource section which provides notes and further avenues for study.

Avronelle

I have named our school 'Avronelle', an old name for the land around a great chalk figure in Sussex – the Long Man of Wilmington. But Avronelle is really somewhere in the Otherworld, somewhere far away, but also very close. It is a place beside the sea, a place that can lead you to cross the threshold between the Known and the Unknown, so that new energy, new ideas can flow into your life as easily as the tide washes back and forth across the shoreline ...

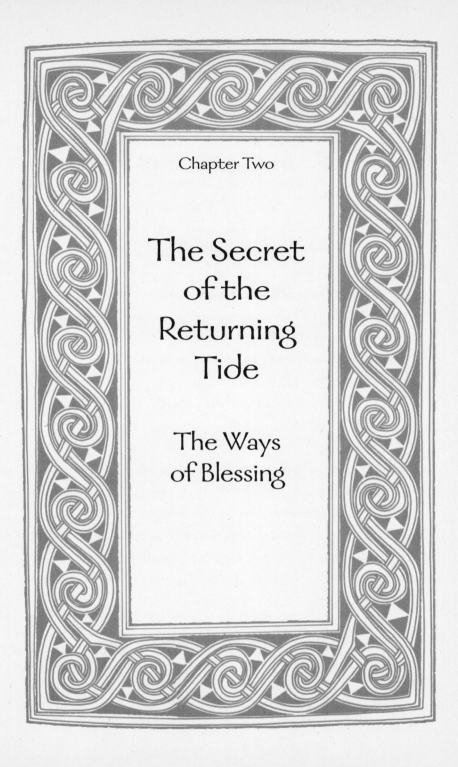

Chapter Two

The Secret of the Returning Tide

The Ways of Blessing

Let me dip thee in the water,
Thou yellow beautiful gem of power!
In water of purest wave,
Which pure was kept by Brighid.

A blessing on the gem,
A blessing on the water,
And a healing of all bodily ailments
To each suffering creature!

from The Silver Bough, (ed. Marian McNeill)

Druidcraft can be seen as both a spiritual path and a path of magic. The art of living well involves knowing how to be both active and passive – how to engage with the world and contribute to it, and how to relax and let life flow around you. It is the same with the art of magic. It involves learning how to be passive or receptive – how to let life's blessings flow effortlessly towards you – and how to be active – how to influence your life positively to become a force for good, for creativity and healing in the world.

The blessing above is an ancient one, and was used in Ireland and Scotland to charge magically both crystals and water for healing. Learning how to bless and be blessed is the first step in learning how to become a magician.

THE BARD'S TALE

Imagine that you have just arrived for the first time at Avronelle. You are shown into a thatched roundhouse, and you seat yourself beside the fire. Gradually, you allow yourself to relax completely. As you do so, a Bard picks up his harp and plays for a while until you feel yourself in that wonderful state halfway between the world of this life and the world of dreams. Then he begins his tale:

The Story of the Selkie

On the islands of the Shetlands and the Outer Hebrides it was considered that a great misfortune would befall you if you ever killed a seal – whether by accident or with ill intent. Seals were thought to be magical creatures that brought blessings to the sea and to the land, and it was even believed that some clans were descended from seals – way back in the distant past when animals and humankind could speak together, and shared the world as one. But there are many tales of humans, both men and women, who in later times enslaved seals and took them as their spouse, to keep their homes and bear them children.

These were no ordinary seals. They were magical creatures part human, part seal and they were known as silkies or selkies. Every year at Midsummer's Eve, or at Bealteinne Eve, a dozen of them would swim ashore at midnight, peeling off their silver skins, leaving them on the rocks, to become men and women for a while, and they would dance together in a circle in the moonlight. This dance would be led by a mysterious old man, a wizard, who would chant and lead the rhythms, until at last the seals would pair off (for there were six males and six females) to make love beside the sea, and beneath the moonlight. Then they would climb back into their silver skins and return to the sea, the women carrying the next brood of selkies within their wombs.

One year an old fisherman, Taggart, had been gathering cockles amongst the rocks, and had fallen asleep on his jacket as the sun was setting. He awoke at midnight to see the mysterious dance taking place in the moonlight, and he was captivated by the selkies' beauty. Each was fair and tall, with fine golden hair. And the eyes of each one shone with a radiance and a knowledge of both land and sea that was as beautiful as it was uncanny.

The dance over, the thirteenth member of the party, the Cunning Man a-centre strode swiftly away from the beach, soon to disappear in the distance. Taggart could hardly believe his eyes when he saw six couples walk hand in hand to different parts of the beach, until at last they lay down together, entwining themselves in warm and passionate embraces. Speechless, with eyes wide and mouth half-open, Taggart watched the scene, until eventually each selkie walked to their little pile of crumpled silver skin that lay on the rocks, climbed into it, at once transforming themselves into a seal which then slid gracefully into the sea, diving and disappearing without trace.

But there was one selkie who could not become a seal again. She looked in vain for her skin, but could not find it. Taggart stepped forward from his hiding place in the rocks, startling her with his sudden appearance. He had hidden her skin, and now held it in his hands. Her clear dark eyes fixed him with a steady gaze and she simply held out her arms to him, and said, 'Please give my skin to me. Without it I cannot return to the sea.'

'Fair woman,' Taggart said, 'Don't go back to the sea. You are so beautiful that I have fallen in love with you, and I want you to be my wife. Stay with me here and marry me.'

'I cannot stay too long on land,' she replied, 'for my skin goes dry and cracks, and I yearn for the sea.' But Taggart insisted, and finally she agreed to stay with him for seven years, so long as she could then return to the sea where she belonged.

Nine months later she bore a child, and Taggart never knew whether he or her selkie partner was the father. But the lad was fine and strong, and the mother and child loved each other with a fierce love that both pleased and troubled the fisherman, who had hidden her skin amongst the cottage thatch.

At the end of her seventh year upon dry land, the selkie asked her husband for her skin. 'I must return to the sea now,' she said sadly, for she loved her son so dearly she could not bear the thought of leaving him, and she even felt a fondness and concern for Taggart, though hardly love.

But to her surprise, Taggart's response was swift and brutal: 'How can you ask this?' he roared. 'Don't you love your husband and child enough to stay with them?'

'Of course I do,' she pleaded, 'but look at my skin – it is peeling and cracking. And look at my eyes that weep continually. If I do not return I will die before long.'

'Nonsense!' said Taggart, who slammed the door and walked towards his boat in a fury. Their son watched his mother sobbing by the kitchen table, and having heard their argument knew what he must do. Without hesitation, he made sure his father was out of sight, then climbed up into the thatch and carefully removed his mother's seal-skin. He marvelled at the way it shone in the sunlight, and at its smoothness to the touch. He ran to his mother and said, 'Here, put this on and go before he returns!'

Looking through tear-stained eyes at her son, she knew he was right and yet she could not bear to leave him. But she followed him as he hurried her to the seashore. There she unbuttoned her dress and let it fall to the sand. At that moment they heard a furious cry of 'No!' and they turned to see Taggart running towards them shouting over and over again 'No! No!'

She looked at her son. 'Go!' he shouted at her – with love not fury. Quickly she stepped into her silver suit, lunged at the water, and within a moment was gone.

But every night thereafter a seal would swim to the shore beside their house and leave two large fish on the flat rocks there. And every night both Taggart and the boy would sit as the sun set to watch the seal arrive, and for a moment the seal would gaze at them with her large dark eyes, and tears would seem to fall from them.

THE COLLOQUY

As the Bard finishes his tale, he plays again upon his harp, until you awake as if from a dream.

'You will find your teacher by the seashore,' he tells the assembled company, and so, without a word, you leave the roundhouse with your fellow pupils and take the path down to the beach. It is evening, and as you walk you can see the moon rising in the sky. You pass the tall Scots pines that lie beyond the last of the houses of Avronelle, and looking back you see their lights twinkling in the growing darkness.

Ahead of you lies wildness and the vast expanse of ocean. You continue walking, down along the steep path through the gorse bushes, until at last you are by the seashore.

Standing alone, her figure outlined by the silver moonlight on the water, is your teacher – Elidir. You and your fellow pupils sit on the smooth rocks around her, and she invites a young man to step forward. His name is Brendan. Elidir unfurls a rug embroidered with Celtic knotwork and together they sit down and begin a conversation – a formal discussion between teacher and pupil that is known as a Colloquy.

'I'm glad you've come here now – on such a beautiful night. This is the best place to learn about the magic of Druidcraft,' begins Elidir. 'Here, at every moment, Nature shows to you the fundamental law of life and of magic – the Law of the Returning Tide.' For a moment, Elidir is silent, and you find yourself watching the gentle surf, listening to the rhythmic sound of the waves upon the beach.

Then Elidir continues. 'The Law of the Returning Tide says that whatever you cast into the sea of life returns to you – often changed, often in an unrecognizable form, but nevertheless what comes to you in your life is usually the direct result of what you have given out into the world. Most people are only vaguely aware of this law, or don't fully accept it, but magicians use it all the time. They deliberately and consciously project positive ideas, energies, images, feelings, thoughts, prayers, chants and spells into the world, knowing fully that they will reap the benefits of these – sometimes quickly but sometimes not for years or even lifetimes. Using your knowledge of this law and the techniques of Druidcraft you can actually work at creating your future lives.'

Brendan speaks: 'Are you saying that peoples' lives are simply the result of their past thoughts and actions – that we all create our own reality?'

Elidir smiles at Brendan, but her smile carries a look of sadness in it, 'I can see that you have thought about this idea,' she says. 'It is true that we do create our own reality – that how we experience the world is made up of how we think, feel and act, and the result of those thoughts, feelings and actions as they play out in our lives. But if you believe that is all there is to reality, then you are accusing most of the people in the world of being responsible for their own suffering – all the adults and children dying of illness or starvation, all the people caught up in genocide and armed conflict, anyone who is suffering in whatever way. The fact is that not only do we create our own reality, but we create other peoples' reality too. Our experience, our lives, are made up of a mixture of influences and events that we have created, and influences and events that others have created as well. It is just too simple to say 'we create our own reality'. We are social and active beings, and we have an effect on the world and the people around us, just as they have an effect on us. So the people in a famine, for example, however much they may be busy creating positive thoughts and feelings, are caught up in a current that is bigger than their own – they are in a group reality caused by the weather, and economic and political conditions. We live in a sea of consciousness and experience, and we often have a great deal of influence over our immediate environment – the patch of sea around us – but sometimes deep ocean currents can sweep us away or change our lives forever.'

She pauses for a moment, as if to gather her thoughts, not looking at Brendan now, but at the ocean, then she continues, 'Once you understand that we create our own reality and are part of a collective reality too, that we each contribute to other people's realities as well as our own, then you can understand the Law of the Returning Tide. It is a law that is played out for us in the world of Nature around us all the time: we reap what we sow, and the harvest from the seeds we have sown is not just ours. This law has been expressed by different spiritual teachers for thousands of years. In the Egyptian *Book of the Dead*, the god Thoth says, "Truth is the harvest scythe. What is sown – love or anger or bitterness – that shall be your bread. The corn is no better than its seed, then let what you plant be good." Thousands of years later, Jesus said, "As ye sow, so shall ye reap." The Eastern idea of karma conveys the same idea: that, to a great extent, our present experience is the consequence of our past thoughts, feelings and actions.

'Druidcraft takes this idea and applies an understanding and practice of magic to it – the idea of consciously sowing seeds for ourselves and others. Once you realize that you help to create other peoples' reality, you become socially and environmentally responsible – and you do magic not only for yourself, but also for others and the world.

'I have used the analogy of the sea and the returning tide, but another useful analogy involves seeing everything in life connected by an invisible web. The old Anglo-Saxon magicians called this "The Web of Wyrd" and the Native American Chief Seattle spoke about the way

"All is Connected". Doing magic involves knowing how to work this web, knowing how to radiate along the web to create beneficial effects for yourself and others. The way we do this in Druidcraft is through the art of blessing. Until you understand the power of blessing this can sound vague and weak. After all, how can simply blessing something make any real difference?'

Brendan says, 'It sounds as if to practise Druidcraft I will have to go around like a priest saying, "Bless you my child".'

'No, no,' smiles Elidir. 'Think of Witches when they say "Blessed Be" to each other. What does that mean? It's simply an archaic way of saying, "Bless you" or "May you be blessed". Think of it another way – think of a blessing as a kiss or a smile. In fact, in Wiccan ceremonies, participants often say "Blessed Be" to each other and then add a kiss. In that way, the term blessing means "love" and "positive energy". The magic that I am talking about is simply the craft of sowing seeds consciously and with love. It is spiritual gardening, where we sow seeds that bring inspiration and joy to others, and where later we harvest the fruit of our sowing – bringing abundance to our lives.

'The idea of blessings is that there is a very real energy or current of beneficent force in the Universe and we can consciously and deliberately acknowledge, honour and utilize this current for the benefit of ourselves and others. Like everything in life, if you ignore something it will tend to go away. If you give it attention, it will tend to come into your life. So it is with this magical current.'

'Yes, but what is it?' asks Brendan.

'You could call it the love of the Goddess or God, or the fundamental building force of Creation, as opposed to the fundamental breaking-down force. Some might even see it as Good, as opposed to Evil. Soon we will explore its source. But whether or not we know what it is, we all know when our life seems blessed, and when it sometimes seems most definitely not blessed! Some clairvoyants say they can tell the difference between objects that have been blessed and those that have not. We believe it is a current that is most definitely real, and that it is also the source of healing.

'Remember a time someone touched you and you could feel the love and warmth in their hands or their embrace? It felt like an energy was coming into you, didn't it? Magic says it *is* an energy and that you can consciously direct it!

'And in radiating this energy, somehow you don't lose energy yourself. Instead, it comes to you in even greater quantities – the more you give the more you receive. This is the Law of the Returning Tide. It is so easy to prove with the phenomenon of the returning smile. Try smiling at someone for no reason. Most often they will smile back. This is just a small example. In a wider sense, the path of magic teaches us that we can radiate blessings effortlessly and joyfully and that, in return, blessings will flow into our life in increasing abundance.

'The returning smile comes back to you fast, but blessings can take years or even lifetimes to reach you. It is vital that you radiate blessings without thought of their return, otherwise they don't really radiate – they stay attached to your ego, to your own needs and desires, and don't seem to travel out into space. The trick is simply to radiate goodwill and positive energy in the knowledge that the Law of the Returning Tide will mean that ultimately you will benefit from them, but that is not your purpose in generating them. You simply let go of any attachment to receiving anything, and enjoy the feeling of giving.

'You see, the art of blessing is just the opposite to the art of cursing. In a nutshell, that's the difference between good and evil magic.

'A magician is someone who realizes that they can consciously direct this force for good or ill. Only foolish or mentally ill people use it to harm; if they were intelligent or sane they would know about the Law of the Returning Tide, and they would know that everything they did would be revisited on them at a later date, often magnified in intensity. That's another law that you'll soon discover – that just as a tidal wave picks up speed and height the further it travels, so the waves of this energy can sometimes increase hugely in intensity over distance and time.

'Think back over your life and you might find that you once did some small thing – smiled, talked to someone, made a decision you thought was minor – and years later you can see that the consequences of this were vast, and have changed your life profoundly. This is how this law works, and that is why it is vital to grasp this at the beginning of your training, otherwise you can make some very silly – and unfortunate – mistakes. The story of the selkie was about this, amongst many other things. It was about the difference between a compassionate and generous approach to life – the one shown by the selkie and her son – and a selfish, grasping attitude – the one shown by Taggart.

'It is a story about being human. We all face dilemmas and sadness in our lives, and somehow we must follow our hearts against all odds. And yet we must still give and bless – as did the Selkie by leaving fish every day on the rocks. In the end, maybe there is no difference in essence between giving and compassion, love and blessing.'

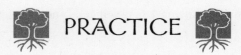 PRACTICE

At the beginning of this chapter we learnt that the path of Druidcraft teaches the art of being magically receptive as well as magically active. As a first step, you might like to open yourself to receiving blessings. As you study this book, you will find that the Goddess Brighid is often mentioned. This is because she is a Goddess of Fire and Water, the Flame and the Well – the two magical and alchemical elements of transformation and transmutation – and she is also a Goddess of Creativity, Poetry and Healing. For this reason she makes an ideal deity to call upon. She is invoked in the blessing of the healing waters and crystal at the start of this chapter, and she is invoked in the following ceremonies that you can perform. If you prefer, you may address the ceremony to another deity, God or Goddess, or simply to 'Spirit' or 'Great Spirit'. The first ceremony helps you to become receptive to blessings; the second develops your ability to actively bless – to actively radiate positive energy out into the world.

SELF-BLESSING AND DEDICATION CEREMONY

Offered here is a self-initiation into the ways of Druidcraft. It is based on an ancient rite, and you can read of its origin in the History section below. You can perform it at home with a bowl of water in place of the sea. But, ideally, you would perform this rite beside the sea on the night of a waxing moon, with a small bonfire on the beach. If you are lucky enough to live near the sea, somewhere that is not freezing cold at night, you could perform the 'Waves of Blessing' part of the ceremony by wading into the sea a little and splashing yourself nine times with handfuls of water scooped from the waves. Read the ceremony through first and decide whether you will perform it clothed or skyclad – 'skyclad' is the beautiful term used in Wicca for being naked, a word derived from the Jain tradition. Your decision may depend on the size of the splashes you plan to give yourself!

If you are enacting the ceremony at home, place a bowl of water and a candle in the centre of your room – these represent fire and water. To create an evocative atmosphere you might want to have other candles lit as well as incense burning. As you enact the ceremony, remember it is the spirit in which you carry out a ritual that is important, not the detail. Give yourself plenty of time to open yourself to the blessings the ceremony is designed to evoke. Pause often and allow yourself to *feel* what is happening to you in your body and soul.

When all is prepared and you are ready, stand beside the fire or candle, facing the moon, whether you can see her or not, and say:

> O Goddess Brighid, Keeper of the Sacred Flame, Guardian
> of the Holy Well, Mother of Song and of Poetry, of the
> Wise and the Gifted, I ask for your blessings on this my
> ceremony. I ask for your blessings on this seeker of the
> ways of magic and of Druidcraft. May I be blessed by the
> power of the earth beneath me, the sea around me, and
> the sky above me!

Stand with your legs spread apart a little now, and stretch out your arms to either side, forming a pentagram shape with your body, and say:

> O Goddess of the Moon, Goddess of the night sky, of
> brilliance and of darkness, please bless this seeker of the
> ways!

Now walk sunwise three times around the bonfire or candle saying three times, with each circling (sunwise is clockwise in the northern hemisphere, and anticlockwise in the southern hemisphere):

> O Goddess of the Flame, Goddess of the Holy Fire that
> burns within my heart and soul and body, bless this seeker
> of the ways!

Now sit, crouch or lie upon the ground and sense your life – and all of your lives – leading to this point. Then, if it feels right to continue, make your commitment to this path by making the following petition and dedication. Or better still, make these statements in your own heartfelt words. In the first paragraph you are speaking to yourself, in the second you are calling to the God and Goddess.

Oh that I could see to the Other Realm – that I could
learn the magic of the Ancients. Oh that the secrets of
the Wise Ones could be whispered in my ears that I
might know their beauty and their power – that I might
love again this land and hear the voices of the Goddess
and the God in the trees and in the rivers.

Oh Goddess of the Flame and Well, God of the Wind
and Sea, of Star and Stone, God and Goddess of all life, I
ask that I might know the ways of Druidcraft, to sow the
seeds of love and beauty in the world and in my life. I will
use the knowledge that I gain, the magic that I learn, to
help and heal, to grow and change. I will nurture the child,
tend the plants and animals around me, foster strength
and courage in the hearts of all.

Now feel your whole life and all your future lives spreading out before
you, and feel a sense of freedom and joy in the infinite possibilities
and adventure that this awareness brings. Then walk to the seashore
or place your hands around the water bowl and say:

Newborn into the ways of magic and of Druidcraft, I ask
for Nine Waves of blessings!

Cup your hands in the sea or in the bowl and splash the water over
you, nine times in succession. With each splash call out a line of the
following blessing, and really allow yourself to receive each blessing
with each wave:

A wave of blessing for my body - may it feel powerful
and free!
A wave of blessing for my voice - may it be strong and clear!
A wave of blessing for my speech - may I be heard
and understood!
A wave of blessing for my livelihood - may I find joy
in my work!
A wave of blessing for my generosity - may it flow from
my heart and hands!
A wave of blessing for my desires - may they be fulfilled
for the greater good of all!
A wave of blessing for my wealth - may my life
be abundant!
A wave of blessing for my health - may it be strong
and vital!
A wave of blessing for my life - may it bring joy and
blessings to others!

Now call out:

Nine waves of grace and of blessing be upon me, waves of
the Giver of Health, Joy and Life!

Give thanks to the God and Goddess for the blessings of this ceremony and, if you are by the sea, finish by meditating beside the fire,
listening to the crackling of the flames and the waves of the sea,
feeling the blessings flowing through your being. If you are indoors,
you might want to meditate, listen to music or enter sleep to allow
the blessings to flow through you unimpeded by everyday thoughts.

A HOME BLESSING CEREMONY

The self-blessing helped you to be magically receptive. The following ceremony helps develop your ability to be magically active.

In order to work magic you have to feel at home in the world – you have to have a sense of centredness, of stability. To achieve this, it helps consciously to bless your home, so that the environment around you feels supportive, protective and clear.

One evening, or day, when the moment feels right, fill a bowl with water and have some incense (unlit to begin with) that you can easily carry around (if incense disturbs your breathing, or if you just don't like it, use a candle instead). When you feel ready to start, decide where the hearth, the centre of your home is, and seated there, close your eyes and imagine you are looking at the Earth from outer space. See it floating in the vastness of the universe, with the sun, moon and stars shining. Then, move down towards the part of the Earth where you live, and imagine you are looking down on the area around your home. Sense the earth and sky, the rivers and stars all sending their special energies to your home and the land around it. Now see your home itself, and imagine a circle of golden light around it. Now come into the home and open your eyes and look around you. Say out loud:

O Great Spirit (or Goddess and/or God), I ask for your
blessings on this my home, my hearth, my household.

Then light the incense or candle and say:

O Brighid, Goddess of hearth and home, I ask that this
incense/flame might be blessed in your name, that it may
purify and cleanse this home, this place.

Then walk through your home waving the smoke from the incense, or
the light from the candle, around the perimeter of each room, working
sunwise (clockwise if you are in the northern hemisphere, or anticlockwise if you are in the southern hemisphere), around the home,
and around each room. Then pick up the bowl of water and say:

O Brighid, Goddess of the well and the flame, I ask that
this water might be consecrated in your name, that it may
cleanse, purify and bless this home.

Then walk through your home sprinkling water from the bowl around
the perimeter of each room, again always sunwise, around the home
and every room. (If you want to be really traditional, and you can get
all around your house outside, then you can sprinkle around the
house nine times, returning to the hearth to light the fire.) Then say:

O Brighid, please bless this house: from site to stay, from
beam to wall, from end to end, from ridge to basement,
from balk to roof-tree, from found to summit, from found
to summit.

Then come to the place that feels most like the centre, the hearth of your home, and sit down and read, or say out loud, the following blessing. And as you do so, imagine that blessings are flowing from Brighid or from Spirit through you, to your house. Feel this energy of blessing actively radiating out into the world through you, as you say:

A blessing upon this home,
A blessing upon this hearth
A blessing upon this ...

(If you have created a sacred space or sanctuary inside or outside your home now is the time to mention it. Use whatever term appeals to you, such as Sanctuary, Sacred Space, Sacred Circle or Place of Transformation/Meditation/Devotion.)

A blessing upon my tallest grass,
A blessing upon my faithful friends,

If you have children say:

A blessing upon my growing daughter/son(s)

Then say:

A blessing upon the household's helpers
A blessing upon my parents,
A blessing upon my occupation.
A blessing upon my goods and income,
A blessing upon my kith and kin,

A blessing upon this place of magic,
A blessing upon my work therein.
A blessing upon me and upon my home in light
or darkness,
Each day and night of my life.

Spend a few moments feeling the blessings invoked infusing your home and your sanctuary, and then sense these blessings radiating outwards to your neighbourhood and to the world, like ripples in a pool. Then, to finish, say out loud:

O Great Spirit/God/Goddess, O Brighid of the Hearth, I
thank you for your blessings.

Blow out the candle, and celebrate!

HISTORY

The crystal blessing given at the beginning of this chapter is a traditional Scottish one, translated from Gaelic, and published in a four-volume collection entitled *The Silver Bough*, edited by the Scottish folklorist Marian McNeill.

Both the ceremonies are based on traditional rites, recorded from the oral tradition in Scotland and beautifully re-worked by the folklorist

Alexander Carmichael in his *Carmina Gadelica – Hymns and Incantations*. Just as Carmichael adapted the original versions, I have adapted his, since any spirituality that is alive has to grow and change – it cannot remain fossilized. *Carmina Gadelica* has been one of the many sources of inspiration for both modern Wicca and Druidry.

The self-blessing is based on a blessing given to newborn children that was undoubtedly originally Druidic. It was used in Ireland as well as Scotland, where it was recorded in the Highlands in its later Christian form. It was still used there until a hundred years ago, and could well be still in use today. Once the baby was born, she or he would be passed over the fire three times, then carried three times, clockwise, around the fire, before receiving nine splashes of water from the mid-wife, who, with each splash, would recite a line of this blessing:

> A small wave for your form
> A small wave for your voice
> A small wave for your speech
> A small wave for your means
> A small wave for your generosity
> A small wave for your appetite
> A small wave for your wealth
> A small wave for your life
> A small wave for your health
> Nine waves of grace upon you,
> Waves of the Giver of Health.

This was the Blessing of the Nine Waves. Nine was a number sacred to the Celts and the Goddess. If you committed a terrible crime, you were placed in a coracle and cast into the sea – beyond the Ninth Wave. To be cast beyond the Ninth Wave meant exile – the worst of all punishments. But within the circle of nine waves you were at home, close to the land of your birth that would always protect and feed you, like the Goddess Herself. I have adapted the words of the ceremony to suit the midwifing not of a baby child, but a baby follower of the Way.

Asking for the threefold blessings of land, sea and sky is deeply rooted in Celtic tradition. Oaths were also sworn on these elements, as is shown in this 'Pledge of the Elements' from Ireland: 'If I break faith with you, may the sky fall on me, may the sea drown me, may the earth rise up and swallow me.'

The second ceremony is based upon two Home Blessings, and again the words have been altered, but only slightly, from Carmichael's versions that can be found in *Carmina Gadelica*.

If you are familiar with Wicca or Druidry, you may wish to perform the initiation within a sacred circle. Here we see some differences in approach: Wicca tends to use a concept of the magic circle drawn from the grimoires of medieval magic, seeing it as a protective device to separate the sacred sphere of operation from the external mundane world. Druidry tends to see the circle as symbolic of all the Earth, rendering the sacred space a microcosm of the whole world. Rather than seeing these as differing concepts, in Druidcraft we can include them both within our practice, the circle both protecting our sacred space from unwanted influences, and at the same time it can be seen as inclusive – creating a microcosm of the macrocosm.

If you are not familiar with circle casting and calling to the quarters, the ceremony will be effective without such additions.

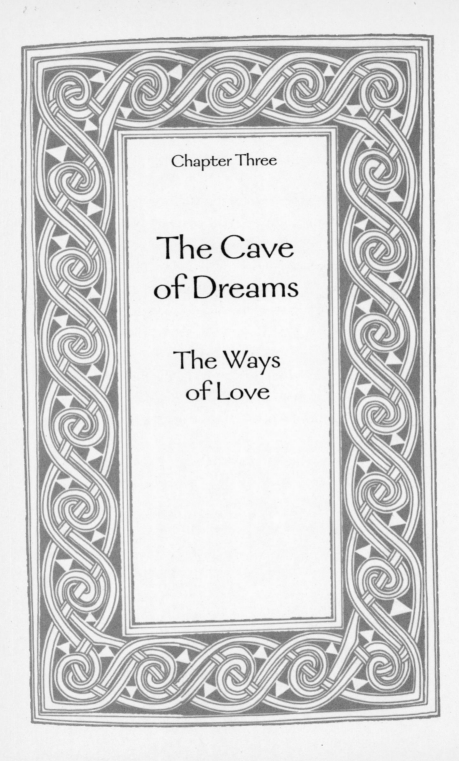

Chapter Three

The Cave
of Dreams

The Ways
of Love

I am the Fertility of the Furrow,
into which you drop the seed of life at planting time.
I am co-creator with the Goddesses and Gods,
bringing forth life from my great and holy bosom.
Boann and Bile
fill my loins with teeming seed and fertile egg,
and the plough carves my image in the sacred form of
the Mother.
Receive I the seed, bear I the life,
creating art, and thought, invention,
and folk in the image of the divine.

OakWyse

At the heart of magic, and of the desire to give and receive blessings, lies the power of love. Romantic love is increasingly emphasized in modern society, but in reality our love can express itself in many ways and one of the tasks of following a spiritual path, and learning about magic, is to broaden our understanding and expression of love. Pursuing a path of nature spirituality, such as Wicca, Druidry or Druidcraft, encourages us to love widely. It fosters a love of the land, the earth, the wild; love of peace and beauty; love of story and myth; love of history and reverence for the ancestors; love of trees, stones, and animals; love of the body and sexuality; love of the sun, moon, stars and sky; love of each other and love of life.

Wicca's great contribution has been to suggest a belief in common with the alchemy of the West and the Taoist and Tantric philosophies of the East, that Creation arises as a result of the love between two aspects of Deity – feminine and masculine, the God and the Goddess. Our world, all of life, comes from this love and is an expression of love. Whenever we express our love we connect to the central force and purpose of Creation. Whenever we make love we re-enact the primal beginnings of Creation. As a result of this belief, creation and sexuality are seen as sacred, and all phases of our sexual lives can be experienced as rites of passage and celebrated with rituals – rituals for birth, puberty, marriage or handfasting, separation and dying. In this way, our sexuality is seen as an integral part of our lives and is honoured, celebrated and enjoyed, rather than being seen as a source of shame. By relating to it in this way, our sexuality becomes a source of energy and healing.

Modern Druidry, in contrast to Wicca, has tended to focus on the product of the union of the two divine principles, on creativity in all its forms. But a study of the old stories of the Bardic tradition show that an understanding of the importance of love and sexuality also existed within the Druid tradition, so that today both Wicca and Druidry are able to share a belief in their sacredness.

THE BARD'S TALE

THE DREAM OF ÆNGUS

In ancient times, the Irish god of Love was known as Aengus Og. Born of the great father-god Dagda and the goddess Boanna of the river Boyne, he was of the fairest face that you could ever gaze upon. Four shining birds flew above his head, and their song was so sweet that whosoever heard its melody would fall in love at once. It was said that each bird was in reality a kiss of Aengus, and in every part of Eire women longed to see the bright wings of these magical creatures hovering beside them, ensuring the imminent arrival of their sweetheart.

Cashel Aengus, the house of the god of Love, was none other than the great temple of New Grange, which lay in the valley of his mother – the goddess Boanna. And it is no wonder that the most magnificent of all temples in Eire should be the palace of the love god – for is not love the most magnificent of powers?

The house of Aengus was constructed from great blocks of granite and white quartz that blazed in the light of the sun, and just as love is born from the womb of the mother as a new child for the Earth, so was the house of Aengus made in the likeness of a woman's womb. And just as the love of man and woman causes a child to be conceived, so did the house of Aengus attract the dawn rays of the Winter Solstice sun, deep into the womb of that sacred hill.

And there, within the hill, while Aengus lay sleeping one night, he dreamt a dream that would haunt him day and night for the next three years. At first in his dream he saw a mighty dragon, and he climbed upon its back and flew to the sun. Then all at once they hurtled towards the Earth, to fly above the waters of a broad, deep lake. And then the vision changed. Aengus was alone upon the lake shore, and walking towards him in dignity and majesty was a woman of such radiance and calm, that he was struck with the deepest passion that man has ever known for woman. He stretched out his hand towards her, and as he did so, his hands and arms became the wings of a swan. And he looked towards her, and she too had grown the wings of such a bird, until all at once they were completely transformed, and they flew as white swans together through the sky, swooping and diving over the lake, before flying westwards towards the setting sun. At that moment he awoke, knowing in his soul that he would not rest until he could find this woman, and hold her close to his heart.

For one whole year Aengus dreamt each night of this maiden, until he was sick with love, and no food would pass his lips. On hearing of her son's illness, Boanna roamed Eire in search of the maiden who was haunting Aengus' dreams, but after yet another year had passed she returned with the like of the maiden not found. And so the god's father, the Dagda, asked the king of the Sidhe of Mumu to search for her. For another full year his men hunted the length and breadth of that green island, until at last they came upon her, walking beside the Lake of the Dragon's Mouth.

Aengus was lifted from his bed and taken by chariot to a castle near the lake. For three days and three nights they feasted, before he was taken to the lake shore. And there they saw one hundred and fifty maidens, walking in pairs beside the water, each pair linked by a silver chain. But there was one fair maiden taller than the rest, who wore a silver necklace, and was joined to her partner by a golden chain.

'It is her! It is her!' cried Aengus. 'She is the maiden of my dreams. She is the lady of my heart!'

But the King of the Sidhe of Mumu led Aengus away. 'That is Yewberry, Caer Ibormeith. You cannot have her. She is of another tribe.'

When the Dagda heard this news, he sent a message to Yewberry's father asking that they meet, but he refused a meeting, saying that he would never give his daughter to Aengus. And so the Dagda and his people attacked his tribe, killing three score men and imprisoning Yewberry's father. Within his dripping dungeon, he was asked once more if he would yield Yewberry to Aengus, but again he refused, saying, 'I cannot, for her power is greater than mine.' When pressed, he revealed that every other year, at the time of Samhuinn, Yewberry became a white swan, along with all the companion maidens that Aengus had seen beside the lake.

Peace and friendship were restored between the Dagda and Yewberry's father, who was released at once, and since Samhuinn approached,

Aengus travelled forthwith to the Lake of the Dragon's Mouth to find, as the sun began to sink low upon the horizon, one hundred and fifty swans gathered upon its still waters. And as he stood on the lake shore he saw the fairest swan of all, adorned with a silver necklace. 'Yewberry! Caer Ibormeith!' he called to her, and she flew to him and he wrapped his arms about her, and as he did so his arms became wings and his body became that of a swan, and they flew together three times around the lake, until, in the last rays of the setting sun, they sped towards his home at Cashel Aengus.

As the two swans alighted upon New Grange, they sang a song of such beauty that all at once the inhabitants of the palace fell into a deep sleep, and for three days and three nights they slept as if in a trance, whilst Aengus and Yewberry lay together in love.

Though Samhuinn ended, their love did not, and they remained as lovers together forever.

THE COLLOQUY

You return with your fellow pupils of the Forest School to the seashore, as once again the moon rises in the night sky. At one end of the beach, you see that a fire is burning beside the entrance to a cave. You walk along the sand and, as you get closer, you see that Elidir is seated beside the fire. She invites you to sit down and for a while she is silent. You sit listening to the sounds of the crackling flames and the crashing waves, feeling the warmth of the fire on your face and body, until at last Elidir turns to Brendan and says,

'If you really want to follow this way, there is no point in working only at the surface – thinking you can burn a few herbs, recite a few spells and then work wonders. To be able to work magic, you have to understand what is at the heart of life, what is driving it.'

Having said this, she leans forward and picks up a stick that has been lying beside her. A cloth has been wrapped around the end of it, soaked in tar. She plunges the stick in the fire and it springs alight at once. 'Come with me,' she says, and you all follow her at once into the cave.

The soft sand soon gives way to pebbles and rocks as you enter further into the cave, which starts gently sloping downwards.

Suddenly Elidir turns around, and shouts, 'Look!' She moves to one side to reveal a skeleton whose bones are half buried in the sand. 'Many people are frightened by seeing skeletons. They worry that that is all we finally are; that death really is the end, and there is no great meaning in life at all.'

'What do you think?' asks Brendan.

'Oh, there's meaning!' she replies, stepping forward a few paces, and holding her torch up high to reveal the back of the cave. And there, on a rocky ledge, are two figures – a man and a woman. They are both about a metre high and are carved out of sections of a broad tree trunk. They are roughly carved, but you can see that the male figure looks a little like the Cerne Abbas giant, complete with erection, and the female figure looks like the Venus of Willendorf – a large full-breasted woman.

Elidir points to the skeleton, then points back at the figures. 'These bones are only here because of their love for each other,' she says firmly, and with that she turns and walks back to the mouth of the cave. You follow her until once more you are seated by the fire.

'Those two figures represent the God and the Goddess – the two great forces that together create life. Ultimately, all of Life is One, but creation only comes about when that One polarizes itself into two energies. In the East they refer to these forces as Yin and Yang. In Druidcraft we talk about them as God and Goddess. In the Qabalah this same idea is expressed in the idea that the Tree of Life has two pillars, with a middle pillar being the place where they unite.'

'This is what lies at the root of life,' Elidir continues. 'This is what the Tantric tradition in the East has been teaching for thousands of years. Of course, many mythologies the world over talk about this too. The Maoris in New Zealand believe that the world was created by the union of the Sky God and the Earth Goddess. When they had children there was no room for them to stand up because their parents were locked in such a passionate embrace that they were trapped, sitting on their mother's stomach! So the eldest brother Tane, god of the trees, stood up and forced their bodies apart – allowing life to flourish on Earth. It is the same idea – that life arises out of the union of God and Goddess.'

'Does that mean that monotheists, such as Christians, are wrong?' asks Brendan.

'Not necessarily,' replies Elidir. 'For instance, electricity is one thing, one force, but it operates by being polarized into two currents:

positive and negative. If you look at it that way you can say that all life is One, therefore there is only one deity who is everything. But this one deity manifests as two complementary or polarized forces, which we can call God and Goddess.'

'But why the erection on the statue? Why the stress on sexuality – surely that's just one level of life – the purely biological. Surely this can't be a spiritual image?' asks Brendan again.

'Have you not seen the images of the Egyptian gods before they were defaced by the prudish French and British who occupied Egypt?' replies Elidir. 'Some escaped their vandalism, and we see images of the god depicted in exactly the same way. And both Druids and Wiccans, like the ancient Egyptians and like the followers of Taoism, Tantra and Hinduism, see sexuality as sacred, not as dirty or evil. People who think the way we make love and the way babies are made is disgusting are simply uneducated. The way love manifests and the way life comes into being is beautiful and sacred – that is why those statues are there.'

Elidir pauses for a while, before continuing: 'Both Witches and Druids believe in reincarnation – that we enter into and out of our lives on Earth many times. And what is the force that drives this educative process? It is sex of course. We only die because we were born. And we were only born because our parents made love. By giving birth to us, our parents ensure that we will die. The act of male and female union is the cause of both birth and death. It drives the process of reincarnation, the Wheel of Life, round and round. And there, at the centre of this wheel of Life, is the God and Goddess, Eternal Mother and Father, united in love, giving birth to Creation.'

'Many of the old Bardic tales speak of the union of God and Goddess, and one of them – the Tale of Taliesin – lies at the heart of the Druid tradition. It is a story about such a union, and of how it gives birth to creativity in the form of the finest bard in the land – Taliesin.

'These stories are precious and sacred, and you can use them to unite the God and Goddess within your own heart – to give birth to the Magician Within, your Creative Self, your own Taliesin.'

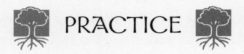

PRACTICE

In the first chapter we learnt about blessing, and being blessed, and Elidir concluded by saying, 'In the end, maybe there is no difference in essence between giving and compassion, love and blessing.'

In this chapter, we have travelled to the heart of these qualities to observe their source in the relationship between two aspects of Deity, between God and Goddess.

These two aspects of the Divine exist within each one of us, and part of the work of becoming a magician, and following a path such as Druidcraft, involves becoming conscious of the God and Goddess Within, and of experiencing their union within our souls. In alchemy this is a process known as the Alchemical Wedding, or the *Coniunctio*.

In Wicca, the union of God and Goddess is enacted by the High Priest and High Priestess during what is known as the Great Rite. The following ceremony works with the concept behind this rite, but does not relate it to the external union of High Priest and High Priestess, but to the alchemical union of God and Goddess within the individual soul. By doing this, we immediately avoid any issues of gender or sexual orientation, whether one has attained the position of High Priest or High Priestess, or whether one even has a partner with whom to enact such a rite. All such concerns become immaterial as we focus on the deeper significance of God and Goddess and their union. This is in the true spirit of the Wiccan Charge of the Goddess which says: *'If that which thou seekest thou findest not within thee, thou wilt never find it without thee. For behold, I have been with thee from the beginning, and I am that which is attained at the end of desire.'*

The ceremony is adapted from the Bealteinne Solo Ceremony of The Order of Bards, Ovates and Druids. The festival of Bealteinne on 1 May in the Northern Hemisphere and 31 October in the Southern Hemisphere is traditionally the time when the union of God and Goddess is celebrated in the pagan round of eight seasonal festivities, but the following rite can be enacted at any time.

THE RITE OF UNION

Take a fairly large candle and fix it within the centre of a bowl. Fill the bowl with water – during the ceremony you will light the candle. Have two candles in normal candlesticks set back a metre from this bowl. These two should be about a metre apart, so that you have formed an equilateral triangle, with a candle at each point. Start your ceremony

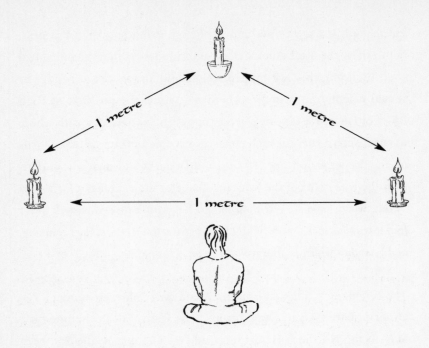

about a metre from the two normal candles, so that the bowl is about two metres ahead of you. Use flowers and incense to enhance your sacred space if you wish.

If you are familiar with casting circles and invoking the four directions, then you might like to do so. Otherwise, simply begin with a prayer such as:

Oh, Goddess of the Flame and Well, God of the Wind and Sea, of Star and Stone, God and Goddess of all life, I ask for your blessings on this my ceremony. I ask for your blessings on this seeker of the ways of magic and of Druidcraft. May I be blessed by the power of the earth beneath me, the sea around me, and the sky above me!

Or you may prefer:

> O Goddess Brighid, Keeper of the Sacred Flame, Guardian
> of the Holy Well, Mother of Song and of Poetry, of the
> Wise and the Gifted, I ask for your blessings on this my
> ceremony. I ask for your blessings on this seeker of the
> ways of magic and of Druidcraft. May I be blessed by the
> power of the earth beneath me, the sea around me, and
> the sky above me!

Sit and meditate for a while on how you came into being. If it feels right, imagine your mother and father behind you, and behind them their mothers and fathers, and so on, so that you form the apex of a great triangle of beings stretching back through generations. Sense how life has travelled through all these beings to come to you. Sense the interplay between Masculine and Feminine, sperm and egg, God and Goddess that has occurred across the millennia. Where did it originate? When did it begin? Allow these unanswerable questions to echo through your being. Then open yourself to the Goddess, the Divine Feminine, to all that the term Woman or Mother means to you and, intuitively, move towards one or other of the candles. Say out loud:

> I turn towards the Moon,
> I open to the Goddess within me.

Light the candle and, as you do so, imagine that you are activating the feminine aspect of your own being. Make a conscious choice to open to this side of your nature, and allow whatever sensations, emotions, images and thoughts to arise without question or judgement.

Give yourself plenty of time, and then, when you're ready, move to the candle across from it and say:

I turn towards the Sun,
I open to the God within me.

Light the candle and, as you do so, imagine that you are activating the masculine aspect of your own being. Make a conscious choice to open to this side of your nature, and allow whatever sensations, emotions, images and thoughts to arise without question or judgement.

Give yourself plenty of time, and then, when you're ready, sit, stand or kneel exactly between the two lit candles and feel the two energies flowing into you, stimulating and awakening their corresponding qualities within your body, your mind and your heart.

You might sense male and female figures to either side of you, or you may become aware of an animal presence on either side of you. You might visualize the two energies as flows of different colours entering you. Do not try to force anything, simply open to the flow of the two energies.

Then, when you feel both energies meeting and merging within your being, slowly cup the hand on the side you have associated with the Feminine, so that it forms a bowl shape, and make a pointing gesture with the fingers of your other hand (one or two fingers extended, the rest folded away). Hold these two positions for as long as you wish, feeling them within your being. Sacred gestures of the hands, such as this, in ritual or meditation are known as *mudras* in the East. Then, slowly and deliberately, lower your pointed finger(s) down into your cupped hand and say:

> I unite the powers of the Sun and Moon within me. With
> my wand I father the Child, with my chalice I mother it.
> Within me lives the alchemy of this union of opposites.
> Let the magical child of my creative nature blossom and
> thrive in the inner and the outer worlds.

Keep your hands in this position for as long as you wish to allow yourself to be fully present to this moment of union. Then separate them and move beyond the two candles and approach the bowl. Light the candle in the bowl, saying:

> The union is complete. May God and Goddess be forever
> united within my soul. May love and blessings, creativity
> and joy flow from my heart, and my hands, my body and
> my whole being. All is One, All is One, All is One.

Meditate or sit in silence for as long as you wish, then finish the ceremony by extinguishing all three candles, saying:

> As the radiance of this ceremony fades, let it remain as a
> light in my heart. May my memory hold what the eye
> and ear have gained.

Then give thanks for the ceremony, saying in these or your own words:

O God and Goddess I give thanks for your blessings and inspiration. This ceremony is ended in the Apparent World. May its inspiration continue within my being.

If you began your ceremony with circle casting, now it is time to uncast the circle.

HISTORY

The fact that the home of the Irish god of Love, Aengus Og, was the megalithic temple of New Grange, is deeply significant. Within New Grange, each year at the Winter Solstice, the Great Rite is performed – a stream of sunlight penetrates to the heart of the temple, through a specially constructed shaft, oriented exactly to the midwinter sunrise. Love, sexuality, creation, birth and the indissoluble relationship between Heaven and Earth, is portrayed in a way that succeeds in uniting the most tangible of elements, stone, with one of the most intangible, light.

Those early ancestors who built the stone monuments that still grace Ireland and the British Isles, understood that the sexual process was sacred and fundamental to all life. New Grange, *Brugh na Boinne*, was clearly built as a symbolic representation of the Goddess, who was fertilized each year by the God at the Winter Solstice. This imagery is repeated at Stonehenge at the time of the Summer Solstice, the first rays penetrating not an enclosed chamber, but a horseshoe, or cauldron, of trilithons. The sexual symbolism of ancient megalithic culture includes the many standing stones that are clearly phallic, and the many barrows that are symbolic of the Goddess' womb.

A Druid altar from the times of the Roman occupation has been discovered in Cumbria, near Hadrian's Wall by the border of England and Scotland, which consists of an upright phallus carved out of a single block of stone. On its side is carved the image of a snake biting an egg. This is exactly the same image that is found depicted by the Native American serpent mounds of North America, the best example of which is in Ohio.

The image of the snake with an egg in its mouth suggests that the ancients knew of the details of conception – with the snake being the sperm and the egg the ovum. Somehow, perhaps intuitively, perhaps through seership, it seems that the Druids and the Native American tribes who constructed the snake mounds, were aware of the mechanics of fertilization. This idea is further supported by ancient rock carvings found in Scotland, that look exactly like views through a microscope of sperm penetrating ova.

The natural rock formations of Australia provide a similar set of symbolic associations for the indigenous peoples of that continent. Male-initiation sites around Uluru in central Australia, for example, are located beside naturally formed phallic outcrops, while female initiation sites are found beside vulva-like cave openings or rock formations. The religion of Ancient Egypt was based upon an understanding of the sacredness of sexuality as was Hinduism, the Taoism of China, the Qabalah of the Middle East and the Alchemy of Europe.

The patriarchal religions of Judaism, Islam and Christianity vigorously opposed such an understanding and introduced cultures of guilt and shame over the pleasures and joys of the body. As a result, sexuality was repressed and distorted, resulting in intense suffering, the repression of women, and punishment for acts of physical enjoyment.

In Europe, as the nineteenth century gave way to the twentieth, many intellectuals began to question the values of their cultures and looked to paganism to provide the inspiration for a spirituality based on a celebration and appreciation of the physical body and its instincts, rather than on a fear and loathing of them. Already, in 1889, the author Edward Carpenter, in *Civilisation, its Cause and Cure*, had expressed the sentiments of this search for a spirituality of freedom and sensuality when he wrote:

> *On the high tops once more man will celebrate, with naked dances, the glory of the human form and the great procession of the stars, and greet the bright horn of the young moon which now, after a hundred centuries, comes back laden with such wondrous association; all the yearnings and the dreams and the wonderment of the generations of mankind, the worship of Astarte and of Diana and Isis; once more in sacred groves will he reunite the passion and the delight of human love, with its deepest feelings of the sanctity and beauty of nature and in the open, standing uncovered to the sun, will adore the emblem of the everlasting splendour which shines within. This same sense of vital perfection and exaltation which can be traced in the early and pre-civilised peoples, only a thousand times intensified, defined, illustrated and purified, will return to irradiate the redeemed and delivered man.*

Here he is suggesting, in florid and exaggerated language, that the early pre-Christian understanding of the sacredness of the human body and of sexuality would return to free and inspire us. This is exactly what has happened in the resurgence of paganism in the last few decades, thanks, to a great extent, to the initiative of Gerald Gardner.

Gardner was the founding father of the modern Witchcraft movement, as Ross Nichols was, in a different way, the founding father of modern Druidry. They probably first met at the Spielplatz Naturist Resort near St Alban's, England during the Second World War. Although nearly 20 years separated them, they shared a fascination with mythology, folk-lore, religion and the occult. And they both loved to talk – endlessly.

Naturism was an idea that evolved in the 1920s as part of the process of the freeing of individuals from outmoded social restrictions that had started to occur following the First World War. It was all part of the move 'back to Nature' in which people sought to escape from the horrors of war, the alienation of city life, and rampant industrialization. They did not want anything, not even clothes, between them and the elemental forces of Nature – water, air and sunlight.

Nichols, a teacher, was a vegetarian and pacifist, and was fascinated by the mythology of Britain. He loved the procession of the seasons through the year, and had published poetry before the war filled with seasonal imagery. Gardner, a retired civil servant, had spent most of his life abroad in Malaya. He was also intrigued by mythology – he was a member of the Folklore Society and had studied indigenous spiritualities in Malaya – and he was a member of the Ancient Order of Druids. Years later, in 1954, his friend Ross also joined the Order.

When Nichols and Gardner met at the Naturist resort of Spielplatz in the 1930s they were already convinced of the dangers of sexual repression. Nichols wrote that Christianity's attitude towards sexuality effectively made it evil, thereby stunting human development. He studied the work of Freud who pioneered an understanding of the importance of sexuality and of the dangers of its repression, and he also read the works of Jung, who was fascinated by alchemy and its understanding of the deeper, sacred nature of sexuality as a vehicle for human spiritual growth and creativity.

Nichols was also interested in the Indian religion of Jainism – he liked its philosophy of non-violence, vegetarianism and non-attachment, and he once wrote that, 'Of the known cultural communities it is the Jains who seem most like a society from which Druidry could have originated.' He then went on to explain their two divisions: those who wear no clothes and are called *Digambara*, which means literally 'clothed in the quarters of the sky', usually translated as 'atmosphere-clad' or 'sky-clad', and those known as *Shvetambara*, translated as 'white-clothed' or 'white-robed'.

Both Nichols and Gardner were convinced of the benefits of Naturism, and had found that freeing oneself of clothes in a natural setting also frees one's mind and spirit. While Gardner took the bold step of introducing a spirituality which took this sense of freedom into its acts of worship, decreeing that Wicca should be practised 'skyclad', Nichols confined his Naturism to his own personal life and when meeting with Druid friends at his private woodland retreat. In his public Druidry he was 'white-robed'.

Gardner firmly believed that the union of God and Goddess lay at the heart of creation, and this theme lies at the heart of Wicca too. Within the Wiccan Great Rite, the union of God and Goddess is enacted either symbolically, through the plunging of the athame (ceremonial dagger) into the chalice, or in reality through the physical union of the High Priestess and High Priest. Some believe that Gardner himself introduced this theme and this rite into Wicca as a result of his knowledge of Tantra and the sexual magic of the Ordo Templi Orientis, since there is no evidence of this practice within folk witchcraft in Britain prior to Gardner.

Even if the Great Rite is a modern addition, pre-Christian culture and spirituality in Britain and Ireland were imbued with an understanding of the centrality and sacredness of sexual union. The 'Ancients wrote it in the Earth', as the Druid saying goes, and the megalithic sites are inherently sexual in their symbolism. In addition, many of the old stories, such as the Dream of Aengus, the Tale of Taliesin, and the story of Kulwch and Olwen, deal with the union between the Masculine and the Feminine.

Gardner intuitively grasped the idea that a spirituality for the New Age, if it was to free itself from the violence and repression of the patriarchal religions, needed to celebrate the body and sexuality, and the union of the Masculine and Feminine principles. The idea did not need importing from the East – it existed already amongst the stones and the mythology of the West.

It is also clear that the Ancients viewed sexuality, love and procreation in the widest sense. Their spiritual and magical life was seen as fostering fertility and abundance at every level, from acts of physical love, to creating fine children, beautiful works of art, abundant crops and healthy livestock. At a cultural level, one of the finest expressions of this was seen in the work of the Bards, who sought the inspiration of the Goddess Ceridwen in Wales, and Brighid in Eire, to incubate poems in the simulated wombs of dark enclosed rooms, from which they would emerge to proclaim their verse.

Nichols, a poet himself, chose to focus on the results of the Divine Union within the soul – creativity in all its forms. Gardner chose to focus on the union. It was as if they each turned their attentions to the side of the equation that best suited their interests and personalities, and now, 50 years later, we can view the situation objectively and see that both approaches, far from being contradictory, actually represent two parts of one whole. Separated, their approaches can be problematic.

Making the sacred marriage of God and Goddess a central focus of Wicca, and the introduction of the idea of skyclad worship, created a number of problems for Gardner and his followers. Wicca became an easy target for the attentions of journalists who would 'expose' naked celebrations and evoke the scandalous image of sexual rites occurring behind the closed curtains of suburbia. This was not helped by self-publicists who capitalized on this interest.

Another, more creative problem arose when those pagans who were not heterosexual objected to the prominence given by Gardner's Wicca to gender polarity. Later writers stressed a symbolic interpretation of this polarity rather than a literal one, saying that the sacred union enacted in the Great Rite need not be of opposite physical genders, but of 'The Masculine' and 'The Feminine' as divine principles, or as inner aspects of the Self. This satisfied some gay and lesbian Wiccans, but once the original idea was discovered not to be an authentic and ancient tradition of Witchcraft, many Wiccans felt free to create versions of Wicca that simply let go of the Great Rite and of the concept of gender polarity altogether. Feminist Wicca, Goddess Wicca, male-only covens and a host of other variations of Wiccan theory and practice developed as a result. In the same way, once the insistence on being skyclad was seen to be not a divine edict but a matter of personal choice, many Wiccans chose to worship robed rather than naked.

Druidry evolved free of such problems. Skyclad Druidry had never been overtly suggested, and Nichols, and most other writers on Druidry, hardly mentioned the issue of sexuality or gender. In addition, gay and lesbian practitioners felt as welcome within Druidry as heterosexuals, as did those who might have felt threatened by the concept of participating in naked celebrations. Journalists could only photograph solemnly robed Druids at Stonehenge, and none bothered to infiltrate Druid groups because no rites involved that subject of perpetual fascination – sex. As a result, Druidry came to be perceived as a rather staid affair and pictures of Druids at Stonehenge, like those of Beefeaters at the Tower of London or students punting at Cambridge, became one of the defining images of British culture.

The downside to Druidry's avoidance of sexuality was that, for some, it came to be perceived as sexless, in contrast to Wicca's obvious sexiness, particularly by those who were free from sexual inhibitions or body-shame. The inherent nature of sexuality in all of life seemed ignored and, as a result, a certain juiciness or *joie de vivre* sometimes appeared lacking in Druidic thought and ceremonial.

In recent times, the picture has changed, and the problems encountered by Wicca in its early days occur less frequently. A wider familiarity with psychological concepts means that a simplistic association of God and Goddess with physical gender is no longer so prevalent. Whereas nakedness and sexuality were explosive issues in the 1950s, they have now become accepted topics of popular culture. Although the majority of Druids, and many Wiccans, prefer to remain clothed, a number of them have discovered that working skyclad, far from encouraging salacious voyeurism, exhibitionism or sexual misconduct, actually engenders a sense of community, of closeness to Nature, and induces feelings of humility, innocence and freedom.

Whether or not the ancient Druids, like the Jains, ever worked naked is debatable and, essentially, immaterial. Druidry is constantly growing and evolving, and the ideals of Naturism espoused by Nichols are in complete agreement with the ideals of Druidry. In addition, a close study of the old Bardic tales suggests a spirituality that is fundamentally alchemical and that shares an understanding of the sacredness of sexuality with traditions such as Taoism and Tantra. The introduction of the theme of the union of God and Goddess into modern Wicca provides an interesting bridge between the two traditions, for if Druidry, in its Bardic tales, can provide the historical underpinning for this central theme of modern Wicca, then one of the key distinctions between the two traditions simply evaporates.

Chapter Four

The Grove of the Summer Stars

The Ways of the Earth and Her Seasons

Three good things in one who loves good health:
enough sleep at Bealtinna (in Spring),
enough food at Meansamhradh (at Mid-Summer),
enough fire at Geamhradh (in the Winter)

Irish Triad

Working with the powers of Nature is one of the central activities of both Druidry and Wicca – and hence of Druidcraft. Knowing how to work with the tides of the Earth, moon and sun is vital if we are to work with Nature and not against Her. When we live in a world of concrete and glass, separated from the cycles and the energies of the natural world, we lose energy and become tired or depressed. But if we can get in touch again with Nature and her seasons, we feel more vital, more joyful. Both Wicca and Druidry celebrate eight times of the year to help us to do this. There are many ways in which we can mark these eight occasions, from complete rituals with others at a sacred site, such as Stonehenge or Glastonbury, to informal ways on our own or with our family and friends. Celebrating these seasonal festivals lies at the heart of Druid, Wiccan and Druidcraft practice, and in this lesson we learn about this eightfold cycle and how we can use the energies of the seasons in practical magic.

THE BARD'S TALE

THE LIFE OF BRIGHID

The great father god of the Druids in Ireland was known as the Dagda. He was a mighty being who possessed a vast cauldron that was so big that whole worlds could be stirred within its depths. To stir the cauldron he carved a great spoon, and a sport amongst the gods was for them to lie together in their father's spoon, while he stirred it round and round the swirling mass of atoms that we call the cosmos.

One night, when lightning streaked the sky and all the heavens seemed to open, the Dagda's daughter was born into the world. No one knows the name of her mother. Perhaps she was the night sky itself or the moon that shines so brightly in our heavens. Perhaps she was the Goddess of the Forest and the deep Earth. Perhaps she came from the constellation of the Great Bear in the Northern skies. Though some whisper that she was Anu, Danu or Dana of the Tuatha de Danaan, in reality we shall never know her name. But out of her womb was born a child of timeless beauty, with flowing golden hair and dark hazel eyes, with strong arms and limbs, and a spirit that was both fiery and as deep as the deepest ocean.

The Dagda knew at once her name. 'We shall call you Brighid!' he declared to the little girl who was born on Earth as the first snowdrops began to appear across the land. With every day that passed her strength and her beauty grew tenfold, until at last she stood before her father as a young woman – a young goddess. 'Let me go out into the world now, Father,' she said to the Dagda. 'Look at my brothers, already they are at work: Ogma inspiring the writings of men and women, Aengus opening their hearts to love, Donn guiding them at death to the Blessed Isles. I too would inspire the hearts of those on Earth.'

Her father replied, 'Your brother Ogma has taught the art of writing and of literature, but you must teach them how to go deeper with their words – how to find the song of their souls. You must teach them how to sing from their hearts. You must introduce the art of poetry to the world.'

This pleased Brighid, for she liked nothing more than giving melody to the spoken word – rhyming and scanning words until they soared and danced in the air before her. But she wanted more. She knew she could give more. 'Give me more tasks to perform, father!' she begged.

'Very well,' he replied. 'Teach them how to give birth not only to poetry but also to themselves. Teach them the arts of the midwife. Show them how to give birth not only to the beauty of language, but also to the beauty of their own bodies. Become the Goddess of Birth, just as your brother Donn is the God of Death.'

'But I want more!' cried Brighid again. 'I can do more, for there is fire in my limbs and my heart and I would help the world and its creatures.'

'If you would help them,' said the Dagda, 'then tend to their ills, care for the sickness of their bodies and souls and become the Goddess of Healing.'

And so it was that Brighid became the Goddess of Poets, Midwives and Healers.

One day, as she went about the Earth touching peoples' hearts with her inspiration, and their bodies with her healing, she came across the great Smith-god Goibniu.

She stood at the door of his forge, entranced by the flames that raged in his furnace. With each beat of his great hammer on the sword that he was forging, Brighid felt a surge in her heart. She too longed to wield a hammer and forge beauty upon an anvil.

Goibniu turned to the door, and seeing her there smiled. He held out his hammer towards her saying, 'Goddess of the Healing Well, you are Goddess of the scourging fire too. No healing may come without the fire of life, no beauty without the well of suffering and rebirth. Come, take my hammer, forge the sword. Make new the world each day!' And with that the Goddess took the hammer and became the Goddess of all Smiths; she would forge iron as well as poems and new births, she would inspire craftsmen as well as poets and midwifes and healers.

And so it was, in the year 455AD at Faughart in County Down, Ireland, that the midwife delivering the baby girl of the Druid Dubhtach and his wife, called upon the blessings of the Goddess Brighid. She picked up the newborn child and, praising Brighid, passed the baby three times over the hearth fire while Dubhtach and his wife watched in joy. Then three times round the fire she carried the child, again calling upon Brighid in thanks and praise. Finally, she brought the little one to her parents, who, kissing the child, nodded in agreement as Dubhtach held up a bowl of water drawn from the Goddess Brighid's holy well close by. The midwife dipped her fingers in the bowl, nine times, and each time she called upon blessings for the child.

They named the girl Brighid in token of their thanks to the Goddess who had given her such health and beauty. Some said that Dubhtach fed her with the milk of cows from the Otherworld. They saw him disappearing into the forest at night with empty pails, and some who followed him reported that they saw him entering a clearing where stood a great cow in a shaft of moonlight. Dubhtach milked this cow until both buckets overflowed, then patting the cow's side he would leave the clearing and it would simply disappear.

As the child grew, the new faith of Christianity spread through the land, until Brighid herself became a Christian, eventually becoming ordained as a nun by the Bishop of Ardagh. She founded a religious community in the shadow of a great oak tree, calling it the Church of the Oak, a name influenced by the faith she was born into – the faith of the oak sages, the Druids.

Such was Brighid's ability to heal, such was the compassion that flowed from her heart, that within a century after she died, she was named a saint. The holy wells of the goddess Brighid became the holy wells of Saint Brighid. The festival of Imbolc on the 1st of February, which had always been sacred to the Goddess Brighid, was now Saint Brighid's Day.

Goddess and saint, human and divine merged in the memory and the understanding of the people. And, as Saint Brighid aged, she aged with the slow turning of the Earth, so that in her youth she was like the warm Spring, appearing first at the dawning of the year in February. Then, dancing to the turning of Spring into Summer at Bealteinne, as her youth turned to middle age, she became known as the mother of souls, some even calling her Foster Mother to Christ. As the summer of her life turned to Autumn, she moved from Bealteinne and High Summer to the time of Lammas, of Lughnasadh, when the harvest was gathered in – the golden corn of the fields matching the golden colour of her hair, which even then shone as brightly in the sunshine as it had when she was a maiden.

Then, as harvest time brought Autumn, so Brighid became the Healer of Souls, the Wise Woman, and as midwife helped others give birth to the children of their love and of their creative spirits, until as Winter stalked the land at Samhuinn, Brighid at last became the Old Woman, the crone, the Cailleach. Finally, in the year 525AD, surrounded by her devoted followers, Saint Brighid passed away, journeying to the Otherworld perhaps to meet not only the Christ to whom she had devoted her life, but the Goddess Brighid with whose name and Spirit she was forever linked.

THE COLLOQUY

At Avronelle there is a Sacred Grove – a place set apart for teaching and for ritual. There seated by the fire in the centre of the Grove is Elidir and she begins her Colloquy with Brendan:

'I wanted us to meet here, to talk to you about one of the most important aspects of Druidcraft. We call our grove here the Grove of the Summer Stars. In the old days, occultists used to think that magic was what went on in a temple, but we believe that magic is what goes on all around us in the world of Nature. And one of the ways we open ourselves to this magic is to celebrate the eight seasonal festivals in places such as this Sacred Grove.'

'Is this the only kind of magic that you work with?' asks Brendan.

'No,' replies Elidir at once, 'there are other kinds of magic, which work at transforming who you are or influencing the world, but I shall speak of these at another time. And as you will discover, it is vital to understand first the kind of magic that I shall tell you about now, because if you want to engage in the kind of practical magic that I will teach you later, you will need to know how to work with the energies of sun, moon and Earth – not against them.'

'So let me tell you about the eight festivals, and as I talk about them I will also teach you a little of the seasonal magic which you will need to know when you come to the work of practical magic in a later lesson.' Elidir then picks up her staff that she had laid on the ground beside her, and draws a circle in the earth in front of Brendan. 'Every six weeks or so, we enact a ceremony, either on our own or with others, to open ourselves to the magic of the time of year we find ourselves in. This makes a yearly cycle of eight ceremonies: the two solstices and the two equinoxes, and the four "cross-quarter" ceremonies as they are called. There are a number of different names for them, but these are the ones we use.'

Elidir then draws what looks like a wheel with eight spokes, and then, as she points to each spoke, she speaks the names and dates of each festival.

'The dates of the solstices and equinoxes are fixed, since they mark definite astronomical events, but the dates that you celebrate the other festivals can vary, since they mark changes of season, which vary a little from place to place, and with changing climate patterns.

'One of the best ways to understand this cycle of eight festivals, is to follow the journey of the Earth Mother, or Mother Nature, around the year. We can begin at any time, of course, because, like the Earth, the year just keeps on going round and round. But let's start at the time

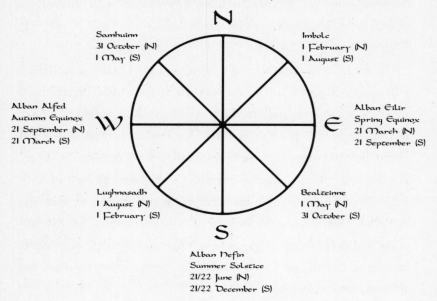

Alban Arthan
Winter Solstice
21/22 December (Northern Hemisphere)
21/22 June (Southern Hemisphere)

N

Samhuinn
31 October (N)
1 May (S)

Imbolc
1 February (N)
1 August (S)

Alban Alfed
Autumn Equinox
21 September (N)
21 March (S)

W

E

Alban Eilir
Spring Equinox
21 March (N)
21 September (S)

Lughnasadh
1 August (N)
1 February (S)

Bealteinne
1 May (N)
31 October (S)

S

Alban Hefin
Summer Solstice
21/22 June (N)
21/22 December (S)

that has come to be known as Brighid's festival, Imbolc – February 1st – the time when Spring just begins to stir in these lands. If you were living in the Southern Hemisphere you would have to reverse all the dates. Imbolc begins there on August 1st.'

'Up in the Northern Hemisphere, at least in Britain, it's freezing in February! Surely Spring doesn't start then?' asks Brendan.

'Keep a look out next February if you don't believe me,' replies Elidir, smiling. 'Spring just begins to tiptoe her way towards us then. The first flowers of the year – snowdrops – begin to appear, and there's a shift in energy beneath the ground as all the plants begin to stir, like creatures slowly coming out of hibernation. Then comes the Spring

Equinox, in March, and Spring is officially with us – even though March can be horribly cold sometimes. Finally, Spring is with us in full force at Bealteinne, on May 1st, when all the blossoms are out and the sap is rising everywhere – even in people!'

'This is the time of the Earth Goddess as the Child growing into the Maiden,' she says, drawing another circle on the ground, cutting it into four like a hot cross bun, with two bold diagonal strokes, and then pointing to the right-hand quarter. Then she continues, 'Just as the moon is born out of darkness, and waxes to full from the merest sliver, so Nature seems reborn at this time, growing out of the darkness of Winter. As warmth increases, plants begin to grow again, and this activity builds until the time of maximum fertility at Bealteinne.

'See if you can sense now, just beyond the grasp of your rational mind, the relationship between Earth, moon and sun. Feel the gradually increasing strength of the sun, as the wheel of the year moves from February to May. And as it moves you can see the land growing greener, the flowers blooming, and animals and people mating. Statistics show that the frequency of mating amongst couples in the Northern Hemisphere is at its highest between March and June, peaking in May, and sexual activity also increases in frequency as the time of the full moon approaches. This whole period – the period of the waxing year – is ruled by the Tide of Sowing. This is the time when Nature urges us to sow, either physical seeds, or the seeds of projects, ideas and feelings, which will grow to fruition in the next phase of the year.'

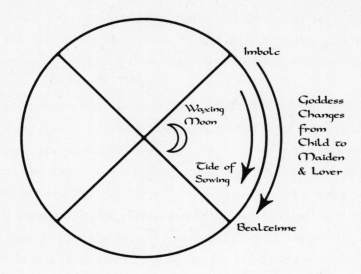

'The next phase,' continues Elidir, 'is ruled by the Tide of Growing – from Spring to Summer. It begins at the time of Bealteinne, which you could also see as the first glimmer of Summer, and it peaks at the time of the Summer Solstice in June, finishing at the time of Lughnasadh on August 1st. This is the time when those seeds that were sown with the previous tide, grow in the belly of the Earth Goddess. She is no longer the Maiden – she has become the Mother. Like the full moon, her womb becomes full, until at Lughnasadh she gives birth, and from her we harvest her crops and her fruit.'

'The first phase of Sowing is good for magic to encourage new projects – whenever anything is new or starting and needs a little help. Now, in this second phase of Growing, we do magic for people or things that

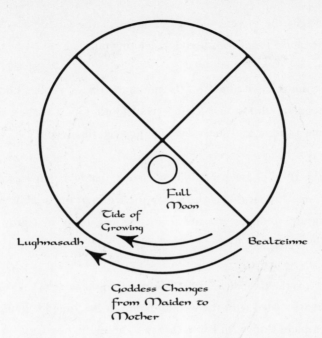

need nourishment and support. It is the time of mothering, so also a good time for doing healing magic.'

'Then comes the third phase, which is ruled by the Tide of Reaping. This starts at Lughnasadh, which marks the beginning of the harvest season, peaks at the Autumn Equinox in September, and finally comes to a close at the end of October at Samhuinn – Hallowe'en. This equates with the time of the waning moon, a time when the Mother has fulfilled her role, and can move into the mature phase of being the Wise Woman – still having the power of the Maiden and Mother within her, but now having the maturity and experience to bring their energies to fruition in wisdom.'

'I thought there were only three faces of the Goddess – Maiden, Mother and Crone?' says Brendan, looking puzzled.

'There aren't three phases of the moon are there?' replies Elidir. 'Ask any woman who is just letting go of motherhood if she's ready to become a Crone, and she'll say, "Not just yet, thank you!"'

'No, this third phase is the time of harvest, that lovely time of Autumn when one can sit down and enjoy the fruits of one's labours of the spring and summer. We aren't ancient yet, we're just grown-up – middle-aged if you like!

'Since it is the time of waning – of the waning powers of the sun – this is also associated with the waning moon. It is a time for doing magic to complete things, to bring things to an ending or fruition. It is a good time for those of us who are hopeless at finishing anything, a good time to divorce or separate too.'

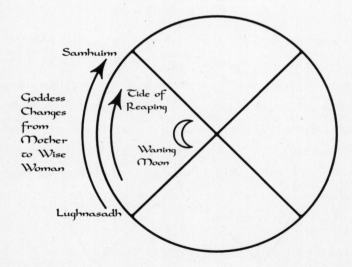

'And the last quarter?' asks Brendan.

'Ah, that is the Dark Time,' Elidir replies, 'the time ruled by the Tide of Death and Renewal. It is the time of the Dark Moon, when you cannot see her in the sky. It begins at Samhuinn in November, peaks at the Winter Solstice in December and finishes at Imbolc when the Goddess is reborn as a child.

'By November everything looks dead – the leaves have been stripped from the trees, the snows come on the high ground. The Goddess walks the land no longer as the Wise Woman, but as the Crone – the Old Woman.

'We avoid doing any magic at this time of the year. It is a time for drawing in our energies, for letting the nourishing power of the dark support us, the way the soil supports a plant through the Winter. And

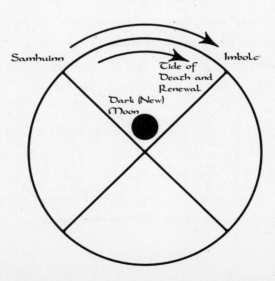

then, of course, Imbolc comes around again and the Goddess of the land is reborn with the first flowers of Spring.'

'But why just the Goddess? What about the God?' asks Brendan, puzzled that the God seems to have been left out completely.

'I am speaking symbolically, not literally,' replies Elidir. 'I could talk about all of this in terms of the God, with him being born as a child at Imbolc, growing into the Youthful Lover by Bealteinne, becoming the Father until the time of harvest at Lughnasadh, then becoming the Wise or Mature Man through the Autumn, until he becomes the Elder through the Winter.

'Or I could remove gender completely and talk about Spring as the Time of the Child growing into the Youthful Lover, Summer as the time of the Parent, Autumn as the time of Maturity and Wisdom, and Winter as the time of the Elder. It is simply that the more you abstract it, the less colourful and evocative it becomes.'

'I understand,' responds Brendan, 'but there's one thing I haven't quite understood. You talked about the phases of the moon and the seasons, but the moon goes through all four phases thirteen times a year, so each season will see all phases of the moon several times.'

'Again I wasn't being literal,' replies Elidir. 'By association, the rising tide of warmth and energy that we experience in the Spring is like the energy and feeling of the waxing moon. The generous strong energy of the moon when it is full is like the time of Summer when there is a sense of maximum energy too. Then, as we decline into Autumn, it's like the decline of the moon in her waning phase. The energy gradually drops down until we enter the dark time of the year, and that's like the time of the Dark Moon, or New Moon as some people call it.

'So, the best time to do magic that needs waxing power, growing power, is in the Spring on a waxing moon. The best time for healing or nurturing magic is in the Summer on a full moon. The best time for magic to help completion and endings is in the Autumn on a waning moon. Then you are working with the flow of the energies of moon, sun and Earth – all flowing in the same direction. But sometimes you cannot wait for the right season to arrive, so you work with the lunar cycle on its own.

'You can see from this that we're working with the power of the seasons magically – with the power of the Earth, sun and moon. But even if you don't want to do any practical magic, you can still celebrate the turning of the year, because by stopping every now and then and taking note of the seasons, by opening up to their gifts, you give yourself a chance to catch up with yourself. Most people are so busy that they don't stop to enjoy life and marvel at the world around them. So, for at least these eight times a year, why not stop for an hour or two and take note of where you are in the great wheel of the year? Open yourself to the energies of Earth, sky, sun, moon and stars and breathe deeply. Celebrate with your family and friends and have a special meal together. And, if you can, do a ceremony that will help to get you back in tune with the rhythm of life and Nature.'

PRACTICE

A BRIGHID CEREMONY

In this ceremony you will be working with the energy of the Goddess. Although this ceremony focuses on the archetype of the Celtic goddess Brighid, feel free to work with another archetype if it suits you better, or simply with a force of feminine healing power. Let your own images/feelings emerge.

Prepare an altar or table on one side of your room or sacred space with snowdrops or other flowers, a bowl of milk, and any other symbols and offerings that you feel appropriate. Also, place on it, or on the floor in front of it, a large wide bowl, full of water, with eight unlit floating candles. Ideally, place your altar in the direction of the North-East. This is not essential, and practical reasons may mean you place it in another direction.

At the centre, light a single candle. You may also have candles lit in the North, South, East and West if you like. Prepare a 'wind instrument' of some sort – if not an actual instrument such as a flute or recorder, a bottle partly full of water to blow on is ideal. Also, find a prayer, poem or reading that praises the Feminine, or the Goddess, that you can use during the ceremony.

When you are ready to begin, sit on the opposite side of your circle or room, so that you are facing your altar across the central candle. If you are familiar with casting circles and invoking the four directions, you might like to do this. Otherwise, simply begin with a prayer such as:

> Oh Goddess of the Flame and Well, God of the Wind
> and Sea, of Star and Stone, God and Goddess of all life, I
> ask for your blessings on this my ceremony. I ask for your
> blessings on this seeker of the ways of magic and of
> Druidcraft. May I be blessed by the power of the earth
> beneath me, the sea around me, and the sky above me!

Or you may prefer:

> O Goddess Brighid, Keeper of the Sacred Flame, Guardian
> of the Holy Well, Mother of Song and of Poetry, of the
> Wise and the Gifted, I ask for your blessings on this my
> ceremony. I ask for your blessings on this seeker of the
> ways of magic and of Druidcraft. May I be blessed by the
> power of the earth beneath me, the sea around me, and
> the sky above me!

Meditate on what in your life needs healing or renewal.

When you're ready, look to the North-East and call to the Goddess in your own words or these:

> Lady of the Waters, Lady of the Flames, Lady of the
> Winds, Bright Lady of the turning Earth, Lady of the

Earth reborn, Maiden and Mother, sweet Bringer of
Light, I call to you.

Then continue with a reading or invocation to the Goddess of your
choice, followed by a silent meditation on Her.

When you are ready, stand and move to the centre, just in front of the
central lit candle. Blow on your flute/bottle and visualize a Gateway
slowly opening. Taking the central candle with you, pass through the
Gateway and sit or kneel before the bowl with the candles. Light them
from the one you have brought. As you light them, visualize or sense
the Lady Brighid appearing before you in the shimmering light. Say:

O Lady Brighid, O Goddess, gentle maiden, bathed in the
white milk of nurturing. The fire of spirit shines through
your eyes. I greet you and bid you welcome, and I ask that
you bless me with your waters of healing and renewal.

Listen to her response; she may wish to tell you something or ask a
question. Allow yourself to feel the blessing of her presence. Allow
yourself to feel healed and renewed.

Dip your fingers in the water, touch your forehead, saying:

Lady, you bless my thoughts.

Then your lips, saying:

Lady, you bless my speech.

Then your heart, saying:

> Lady, you bless my feelings.

Then your genitals, saying:

> Lady, you bless my desires.

Then the ground, saying:

> Lady, you bless my life.

Repeat and/or expand these words and actions as you feel.

Listen for any further message the Lady may have for you. When you are ready, give your thanks and say your farewells. Extinguish the candles in the bowl, and return to the centre of your circle carrying the central candle, still alight. Stand, facing the Gateway, and say:

> I thank you Lady for your blessings on my life. Though I now close this gateway [gesture to close the gate] I know that your radiance continues to flow through me.

Now extinguish the central candle and say:

> As the radiance of this ceremony fades, let it remain as a light in my heart. May my memory hold what the eye and ear have gained.

Then give thanks for the ceremony, saying in these or your own words:

> O God and Goddess I give thanks for your blessings and inspiration. This ceremony is ended in the Apparent World. May its inspiration continue within my being.

If you began your ceremony with circle casting now it is time to uncast the circle.

HISTORY

Celebrating the eight festivals has become the cornerstone of modern pagan practice. Witches, Wiccans and Druids all celebrate these times of the year. Although we can find traces and records of ancient practices and folklore associated with these special times, we cannot be sure that any particular community in ancient times celebrated all eight. In the modern era, it was only in the middle of the last century that Ross Nichols and Gerald Gardner introduced the celebration of the complete eightfold cycle – a practice that has now become widespread. Both men were members of the Ancient Druid Order, but found that their fellow Druids only celebrated the Summer Solstice and the two equinoxes. When Nichols founded the Order of Bards, Ovates and Druids in 1964 he introduced a celebration of the Winter Solstice and the four Celtic fire festivals. Since then, most Druids observe all eight special times. Gardner's coven began celebrating the eightfold cycle in the mid-1950s, combining the four Celtic Fire Festivals, or Sabbats as they are called in Wicca, with solstice and equinox rites.

Both men were discussing the importance and value of celebrating these times from the 1930s onwards. Gardner wrote about them in his book, *The Meaning of Witchcraft*:

> *The Witches and the Druids certainly share a number of beliefs: a belief in a future life and in reincarnation; in the efficacy of the magic circle; in forms of prophecy (or, as we would call it, clairvoyance); in the sacredness of Stonehenge and other stone circles, which in later times became the traditional meeting-places of Witches; and in an acute dislike of committing their teachings to writing. But perhaps the most striking link between the Druids and the Witches is that of the four great ritual occasions the Witches call 'Sabbats'.*

In practice, those four occasions became eight when Gardner decided to include the solstice and equinox celebrations in the Witches' calendar.

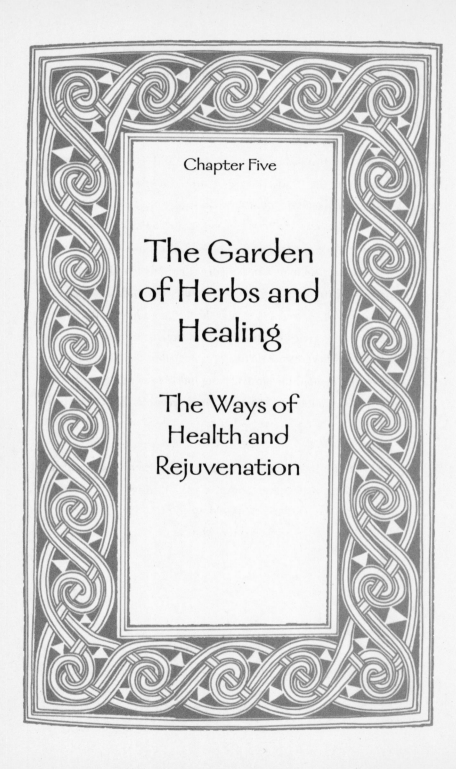

Chapter Five

The Garden of Herbs and Healing

The Ways of Health and Rejuvenation

The island stretched smooth to the eye, sweetly sound; in its
midst was a lake, and many sheep within a paling. From the
sea swept a great eagle of fierce flight; branch in its talons, it
landed by the lake verge. Other fine birds stripped the
wondrous tree, its branches imparting the virtue of redness
to the waters.

Joyfully they greeted the wondrous eagle, the noblest of birds,
valiantly come to that place. The great bird dived into the
lake, its years unburdening; it rose again in youth's vigour,
stronger than ever before. Diuran the Bard also dived in;
no rash leap this, his body remains in finest fettle, without
loss of hair or teeth.

from The Voyage of Maelduin, (8th-century Irish),
trans. Caitlin Matthews

In ancient times, Witches and Druids undoubtedly developed many ways in which to preserve health and long life. Some would have worked, and others not, but today we have a unique opportunity. If we are open-minded enough we can draw on the methods of the ancients *and* on the knowledge of modern science. In doing so, we can develop ways of health and healing that are not grounded on the superstition of the past, or the misguided worship of modern scientific reduction-ism, but instead on ways that understand the workings of Nature – ways that work with Her, rather than battle against Her.

THE BARD'S TALE

AIRMID'S CLOAK

The story I will tell you comes from the land of Ireland. Imagine you are in the Mead Hall of Tara. You can see the King and Queen sitting at the High Table. And there, seated to the right of the King, you notice his Chief Druid – tall, with flowing beard and wise face. He is deep in counsel with the King. The bard shakes his golden stick, covered with bells, which jangle merrily. A hush descends upon the company, and the bard begins playing his harp.

After a while, the bard stops playing, and begins his tale: 'I am going to tell you,' he says, 'why we are not immortal and why sometimes the doctors cannot cure us. It all happened long ago, when the gods walked with us in these lands. The God of Healing was known as Diancecht and he was a strong and powerful man with dark brown eyes, long hair and a great beard that grew to his waist. Such a healer was he that his hands could seal wounds simply with a touch, and his voice could cure the ills of the soul simply with a song. But he was a man in great demand, and he was a man with a temper.

'One day he heard someone remark that his son Miach was a better healer than himself. He shrugged off this comment. He had trained the boy himself, and knew that no one was better at the healing arts than the great Diancecht. But over the coming weeks and months he started to hear more and more rumours and reports that his son had indeed surpassed him – that Miach rather than he should now be known as the God of Healing. In a fit of fury, and without thinking, Diancecht found his son and struck at his head with a sword. Miach instantly healed the sword wound on his neck. So Diancecht struck him again, harder, cutting him to the very bone. Again, Miach healed himself in an instant.

'A third time the great God of Healing picked up his sword and this time he struck at the top of his son's head, breaking through his skull and cutting into his brain. But once again Miach was able to heal the wound. Finally, Diancecht raised his sword for the fourth time and striking Miach's head he cleaved his son's skull and brain in two. Even the greatest healer could not have cured himself, let alone another. So Miach died there and then, in his father's arms. Diancecht's tears of sorrow and regret at his foolish pride and jealousy mingled with the blood of his own child whose soul had already departed for the Summerlands.

'Still weeping, Diancecht dug a grave and placed his son's body in it, covering it with earth as he said a prayer for his son's soul on its journey to the Otherworld.

'The following Spring, a miracle occurred. Where Miach had been buried, there grew a herb garden – no ordinary garden this, but a garden in the shape of Miach's body. And from this shape there sprang three hundred and sixty-five different plants, each one a cure for the illnesses of the three hundred and sixty-five nerves of the human body.

'Miach's sister, Airmid, discovered the miracle whilst visiting her brother's grave. She realized that Miach had found a way to convey his healing knowledge to the world. She decided at once to preserve this knowledge for all time by gathering the herbs and laying them out on her cloak, which she spread beside the grave. As she picked each plant, she placed it carefully in the right position upon her cloak, until at last she had the form of her brother, laid out in flowers and leaves beneath her feet. She then planned to let the herbs dry, whilst she catalogued each one, relating it to the part of the body upon which it lay, until at last she would possess a complete apothecary that could cure every known ailment. But this was not to be. Although her father Diancecht sorely regretted killing his own son, he was still a jealous god who could countenance no rivalry. He discovered Airmid beside the grave, just as she laid the last herb upon her cloak. At once, he understood her plan and, in a fit of jealous rage, he grabbed hold of the cloak, lifted it up, and shook it furiously, scattering the herbs to the four winds.

'And that', said the Bard, beginning to play again upon his harp, 'is the reason why our healers – however skilled they might be – may sometimes be unable to cure you of your ills. And that is why, in the end, each of us must die, since the knowledge of the herbs of healing and rejuvenation has been lost with the death of Miach.'

THE COLLOQUY (PART I)

It is time to learn about Health and Healing. You meet Elidir outside the roundhouse of the Hedge School and with your fellow pupils you take a narrow path that leads away from the gardens around the school, towards a part of the land where members of the community attached to the school live. Amongst the trees and hedgerows you start to see a number of small wooden houses, each with its own garden, and each looking very different. Some are painted in bright colours, others in earthy pastel shades, while others are finished simply in stained or varnished wood.

Elidir stops and gestures toward the houses, 'You see you cannot separate the way you live from the whole subject of healing. People think that they can live in concrete boxes, isolated from Nature, eating food that was harvested months before and mummified with preservatives, and still be healthy. Here we believe that to be really healthy you need to live close to the earth. That is why none of the houses here are more than two storeys high. The earth gives off energy that feeds our energy-bodies. And food contains this life force too, but not if it has been tampered with, added to or stored for too long. So the first things we do to ensure our health and to live longer are to have our homes close to the earth, ideally with no concrete beneath us, and wherever possible to eat food that we grow ourselves.

'Look at the houses – notice how many windows they have. We believe in the energizing power of the four elements – earth, air, fire and water – so we want our homes to have as much air and sunlight as possible, as well as earth-vibrations. And we get our water energy from the rain and the stream that runs through the land here.'

Elidir then walks on and, as the group follows her, you notice that the houses have big windows, with decks that run straight from them to the garden outside, where there is always a pool. Some of the gardens are lucky enough to have the stream that she has mentioned running through them. Each house also has solar panels on its roof, and a small wind generator.

Eventually, you turn a corner and there ahead of you is the herb garden. In the centre is a large bed of herbs laid out in the form of a pentagram. Elidir invites you all to be seated, and summons Brendan forward to engage in the Colloquy.

'No doubt you know about this symbol?' she asks him.

'Only a little,' he replies.

'It is the perfect symbol to have in a healing garden, because it is a symbol of the human being. Lie down here on the grass,' Elidir says to Brendan, who at once lies down.

'Spread your arms and legs out. Spread-eagle yourself,' says Elidir firmly, as she begins gathering pebbles from the path. She then places one under each of Brendan's feet, one by each of his hands, and one above the top of his head. 'Now get up!' she tells him.

As you look at the five stones that remain on the grass, Elidir takes a stick and slowly traces a line from one stone to the other, until you can see that indeed she has created a pentagram – a five-pointed star.

'In addition to this figure symbolizing the human being,' Elidir begins, 'it also symbolizes the five magical elements we are made of – earth, water, air, fire and spirit.'

'And it symbolizes the five senses too, doesn't it?' asks Brendan.

'It does indeed. All in all a finely drawn pentagram is just the right symbol for the healthy, balanced human being, which is why so many of us wear pentacles.' After a pause, Elidir continues, 'Now I'd like to talk to you about the Bard's tale you have just heard. In symbolic form, it is really the story of the origin of our craft, for we believe we are slowly reclaiming the lost knowledge of Miach. Like Airmid, we are gradually piecing together a puzzle, and, of course, all the herbalists in the world have also been doing this.

'And here,' she says, gesturing around her, 'is the result of our work. Over there is meadowsweet, used to soothe fevers and as a natural painkiller. And there is vervain, the most important herb for Druids. It lowers fever, eases headaches, cleanses the liver and kidneys, and can work wonders for eczema, rheumatism and ear infections. To know how to use these herbs requires skill and knowledge that you can obtain by studying in our College of Healing. Nevertheless, you can begin right away to work with herbs if you would like to.

'The first thing you must know is that unlike conventional medical science, our healing work is rooted in a spiritual, magical understanding of the world. We believe that as humans we are in essence Divine, and that true healing comes from this Divine centre within us. In other words, it comes from the God or Goddess. So, when you pick a herb, make a remedy or administer it, say a prayer to the Divine – to God, Goddess or both of them.

'Here is a prayer that comes from a twelfth-century English Herbal. You can see that even at that time the old herbalists and healers were praying to the Goddess for their cures. Listen to it, and imagine you have just prepared an elixir of herbs for your patient, and that you are praying to the Goddess for it to work.'

> *Earth, divine goddess, Mother Nature, who dost generate all things and bringest forth ever anew the sun which thou hast given to the nations; Guardian of sky and sea and of all Gods and powers; through thy influence all nature is hushed and sinks to sleep.*
>
> *Again, when it pleases thee, thou sendest forth the glad daylight and nurturest life with thine eternal surety; and when the spirit of man passes, to thee it returns. Thou indeed art rightly named Great Mother of the Gods; Victory is in thy divine name. Thou art the source of the strength of peoples and gods; without thee nothing can either be born or made perfect; thou art mighty, Queen of the Gods. Goddess, I adore thee as divine, I invoke thy name; vouchsafe to grant that which I ask of thee, so shall I return thanks to thy godhead, with the faith that is thy due.*

> *Now also I make intercession to you, all ye powers and herbs, and*
> *to your majesty: I beseech you, whom Earth the universal parent*
> *hath borne and given as a medicine of health to all peoples and*
> *hath put majesty upon, be now of the most benefit to humankind.*
> *This I pray and beseech you: be present here with your virtues, for*
> *she who created you hath herself undertaken that I may call you*
> *with the good will of him on whom the art of medicine was*
> *bestowed; therefore grant for health's sake good medicine by grace*
> *of these powers aforesaid.*

'You can use such a prayer, or you can say the same thing in your own words, conveying the essential meaning, which is:

> Dear Goddess, please bless this plant, fill it with your
> powers, and grant healing to whomever is your patient.

'Now, the time you pick a herb is most important,' Elidir continues, changing the subject. 'The powers in a plant vary according to the time of day, the phases of the moon and even the position of the stars. Of course, they vary greatly in accordance with their own life cycle. You do not want to pick them before they have reached their full strength or when their strength is waning. You will have to learn this knowledge slowly, but as a general rule follow your common sense and intuition. If a plant feels "unripe" or "feeble" as you hold your hand above it, leave it alone and find one that feels right. Pick it early in the morning, with the dew fresh upon it, and try to pick it on a waxing moon, when its powers will be rising.

'The Witches and Druids of old placed great importance on the moment of picking, because it is at that moment that you "kill" the plant. It sacrifices its life for you and the healing power of that life is transferred to your remedy and through that remedy to your patient.

'So, it is appropriate – and necessary – to say a prayer. If you don't need the whole plant, but only a few leaves or berries, it is still handing you little packages of its life, and you should still say a prayer. As you pluck the plant, sense the life in it and thank the Goddess for the gift of that life.

'Let your herbs dry in the sun, rather than artificially. Everyone who practises Druidcraft should grow vervain. Even if you don't have a garden you can grow it in a window box or in a small pot. Use the dried leaves like tea leaves to make a drink that will cleanse you, and when you perform ceremonies use the dried leaves as incense. Vervain is the equivalent of the sage that is used by many Native Americans in their ceremonies. It is purifying and cleansing, so you can waft its smoke around your magic circle, and around the auras of those who are working with you. It is good to have sprigs of it on your altar too, and you should change them regularly.'

Elidir then points to the trees that surround the herb garden, the gnarled old oaks, weeping willows, birches and beech trees. 'Every living thing – stone, star, tree, animal, flower, stem, leaf – they all bring us gifts of life and energy, and in Druidcraft we learn how we can receive these gifts and, in our turn, pass on these gifts of life, inspiration and healing to others.

'When you are feeling good, you have energy flowing through you, and when you are feeling ill or low, it feels as if you have no energy. One of the great benefits of working in this way is that you can learn how to collect, store and intensify the energy in your body. The Druids call this energy Nwyfre, (pronounced Ne-wee-frey) which comes from an old Celtic word for 'Firmament'. In Yoga this force is called "prana", in Sufism "baraka". Some people simply call it "life force".

'Nwyfre is in all living things and in every part of Nature, and in certain places it is stronger than in others. That is why particular places have developed over the years as "power points" or healing centres – the Earth's magnetism varies in intensity at different places, and so does the level of negative ions. Places such as the seaside, waterfalls and mountains have more negative ions in their atmosphere, and they contain high levels of Nwyfre, which is why people visit these places to feel better. There are other places that drain us of energy. Usually these are places that have banished Nature, such as high-rise offices with air conditioning and neon lighting, or places that feel "used up" or "worn out". Sometimes there are places that feel worse than that, perhaps because something awful has happened there and the tragedy still lingers in the atmosphere.

'Nwyfre is also in food. The sooner you eat food after it is picked from the ground or the tree the better, because the longer it is stored, the more the life force drains away from it. Also, the more it is processed, the more Nwyfre it loses. That is why you should grow at least some of your own food.'

'But I don't have the time or space to do that Elidir,' says Brendan.

'Oh, but you do,' she says, inviting you all to follow her. Soon you reach a small house lying on the edge of the herb garden. 'This is where I live, and I want to show you how you can get a good supply of Nwyfre every day, even if you don't have a garden or much time.' She then shows you into her kitchen.

'Look here!' she says, pointing to a row of jars and pots on the window ledge beside the sink. In the jars are beans in various stages of sprouting. The tops of the jars are covered in muslin, secured by rubber bands. 'Just throw a handful of alfalfa seeds in one jar, mung beans in another, rinse them with water every day, and in only four days you can be eating sprouts that are bursting with vitamins and minerals.'

'But the ancient Witches or Druids didn't do this!' says Brendan.

'Who says we're trying to live like exactly like them? What we're doing here is living with the inspiration and the ethos of our spiritual ancestors, but in every age we must create the spirituality that answers to the needs and Spirit of the times. If we could summon up a wise old Druid or Witch from ancient times and explain the benefits of eating these things, I think she'd agree with us, don't you? Remember Airmid's task of piecing together the puzzle? All our lives we should adopt that approach – of adding to our store of knowledge of how to live wisely, fully, passionately, and then to pass on that store to our children.

'Now, if you've got a little more space and time you can add a few pots of earth to your miniature farm. Bury a few garlic cloves in one pot, and grow parsley and chives in others. As they grow, snip off a few shoots with a pair of scissors and add them to your sprouts when you have a salad. You can also grow lentil sprouts in earth in this way, and use beets and onions to generate green shoots too. All of these will generate fresh green shoots full of minerals and vitamins every few days. If you have a salad every day made of these home-grown greens your health will benefit enormously. You can also grow herbs indoors – basil, thyme, marjoram, balm, borage, caraway, chervil, coriander, dill, rosemary and savory, amongst others. Children love helping with this – they can see the magic of life growing in front of their eyes.'

Elidir now changes tack: 'But not eating every now and then is as important as eating!' Having said this, she leads you all out of the kitchen, through the garden and towards an orchard that lies at the western side of the herb garden.

As you approach the orchard, you see that it is devoted to growing apples. She plucks one from a tree, and says, 'Look!' She takes a knife from her pocket and cuts it sideways in two. There in the centre of the apple is a perfect pentagram with the apple seeds embedded within it. 'The Druids believe the apple was given to us by the gods – it is the food of paradise, of the Summerlands where we go when we die. That is why it is blessed with the seal of the pentagram at its core. Every year, as the Autumn approaches, many of us at Avronelle undertake a cleansing fast to prepare us for Winter and build up a store of Nwyfre inside us. We eat only apples for three days, that's all! Every time we feel hungry we just eat an apple or two. The soft fibre in the apple acts as a cleanser to our intestines and colon, and the juice provides us with essential minerals and vitamins. Some members of the community press the apples to make juice and they drink that as well as eating the apples. Others like to include raw hazelnuts in the diet – they like the protein and extra minerals they bring, and hazelnuts are another sacred food of the ancient Druids. So, by combining apples with hazelnuts they feel they are eating "the food of the gods". As you can see, we have quite a different relationship to the apple from many Christians who believe Eve used it to tempt Adam. If you ever want to try this, just make sure the apples are not sprayed with chemicals. You don't want to spend three days eating pesticides.

'What tends to happen nowadays is that there is so little Nwyfre in processed food and drinks, that we eat and drink more and more of them in a desperate attempt to get the life force we need. Instead, it is much better to break the pattern by having a "mono-fast" such as this for several days, and then to start eating in a healthier way – with as much raw food as possible. Cooking tends to remove a lot of the vitamins from food, and the fibre and plant enzymes work better inside us if they have not been subject to vigorous boiling or frying.'

'What about meat? Do you think we should become vegetarians?' asks Brendan.

'The wonderful thing about a way such as this is that it is a way of life that you craft for yourself. It is not a religion that lays down the law about how you should behave. It is a way of life, and a way of working magically, that helps you to find the source of your own power and your own understanding of life. For most people, as they contact that power and that understanding deep within them, they discover a growing reverence for life and a desire to live in as simple and natural a way as possible. So, many people who follow this path are vegetarian because they feel it is wrong to kill animals, and they point to all the health problems associated with eating meat. But others believe that compassionate farming is the answer. Many of them have tried vegetarianism and have found it doesn't suit them. We would all like to be told what to do, but it seems that each of us has to find out what our body needs and what gives it the best health and the most energy. I'm afraid it is one of those issues that only you can discover the answer to.'

'Tell me more about Nwyfre. It sounds such an important concept,' asks Brendan.

'I have explained how we get Nwyfre from food,' Elidir begins, 'Now let me tell you how we get it from other sources. The pentagram can help us again.' Pointing to the star in the centre of the apple, she continues, 'We get a great deal of energy from the four elements, and from the fifth element of Spirit, which is present in all the other elements, but most of us don't consciously draw in this energy. Once you use your consciousness, it makes all the difference. I presume you have heard about the energy centres of the body?'

'You mean the chakras?' asks Brendan.

'Yes, that's the term for them in the East. We just call them energy centres. Well, the whole body is an energy centre in as much as we receive and give off energy from our whole bodies. Physiologists can measure part of this energy as bio-electrical discharges from our body, and an engineer called Semyon Kirlian developed a camera that can photograph these discharges. But there are certain parts of our body which seem to act as specialized energy receptors and distributors. Good healers know how to work with these centres to cleanse and balance them, but there is a way each of us can do this for ourselves to a good extent and that is by using Nature and the elements.'

Having said this, Elidir gestures for you all to stand. She says, 'One experience is worth a thousand words, so follow me!' With that she walks back towards the roundhouse, following the path beside the pentagram herb bed, and back through the winding lane that leads past the houses and gardens.

Rather than continuing on to the roundhouse, Elidir leads you through a small gate to one side of the path, and you follow her until finally you arrive at a secluded garden, bathed in sunshine. In the midst of the garden is a wooden pavilion and she leads you straight towards it. Opening the door, she ushers you in. There is a wonderful atmosphere in the room. Sunlight streams through the open windows, there is a smell of fresh flowers and herbs, and in the centre of the room stands a harp beside a low couch. Elidir asks you to sit around the sides of the room, while to Brendan she says, 'Why don't you lie down here, and I'll take you through a healing meditation we use to bring energy to our bodies – to recharge and balance ourselves by taking in more Nwyfre.'

Elidir begins to play the harp, and over the sound of her music she says, 'The harp is the most healing instrument on Earth. That is why the bards of old not only used the harp to tell tales, but also to heal people. As you listen to the music, just let go of all your cares and concerns. Allow them to float away with the music.'

 THE PRACTICE

To carry out the following exercise, you will either need to have a friend read it out to you as you lie down and listen to it, or you can read it through, remember the sequence, then carry it out from memory. Alternatively, you can record it yourself on to a tape recorder, or order a CD version of it from the Order of Bards, Ovates and Druids (*see* page 163).

THE BLESSING OF THE ELEMENTS

To begin, either listen to some harp music or imagine it playing as you lie on your floor or bed. Then, when it finishes, focus on your breathing. Become aware of yourself breathing in and out, and as you breathe in, feel yourself breathing in energy, calm and tranquillity. As you breathe out, feel all your tensions and anxieties falling away from you.

Do this for as long as you wish, just breathing in and breathing out.

Then become aware of the earth beneath you. Feel its energy rising up into your body, and as you feel this energy rising up, it is as if you can feel yourself sinking down. Just relax and let go, allowing yourself to feel at one with the earth, at one with the rich dark soil, with the rocks and stones of the earth, with the crystals and precious stones within the soil. Experience this for as long as you like.

Then, feeling energized and calmed, grounded and invigorated, you become aware again of lying on the earth.

In your imagination, sit up slowly. There ahead of you is a lake of crystalline water. Imagine diving into the lake. Feel the water on your skin, on your hair. Feel how the water supports you and at the same time invites you to sink deeper into its mysteries, its life. You find yourself swimming down into the depths of the lake and, miraculously, you discover that you can breathe underwater easily. You find an underwater cave near the bottom of the lake, and you swim into it, finding that it becomes a passage, a tunnel, that leads you out into the ocean. Passing brilliantly coloured fish and coral, you swim to the surface and leap like a flying fish up into the sky, which is as blue as the water that now lies below you. Then you splash down into the sea, enjoying the feeling of your body meeting the water, swimming down into the ocean, hearing the sound of whales and dolphins, which you can see in the distance through the blue depths. Open yourself to all the power and wonder that swimming in the ocean brings to you – all the wildness and the beauty – then swim back through the underwater tunnel, out of the cave and into the lake. Feel the gentler, calmer energy that the lake brings to you, and then climb out and lie down on the shore, sensing yourself invigorated and energized, calmed and centred.

After a while, with your eyes closed, you start to feel the gentlest breeze on your face and body. It feels so good. Now, in your imagination, open your eyes and look up into the sky. It is a perfect azure blue, with one or two clouds drifting gently by. Allow yourself to breathe in the energy and the clarity of the sky. As you breathe the energy of the sky into your body, you feel as if you are floating up into the air, as if you are as light as a feather. Drift up towards one of those white clouds and float on to it.

Now just lie back on the soft white cloud. It is like the softest bed in the world. When you look up, you see the deepest blue sky above you. Soak in this blue colour, let it flow over you and through you.

Stay with this experience for as long as you like, and then feel the cloud slowly landing beside the lake shore. Climb off the cloud, and lie beside the lake, while the cloud drifts back up into the sky.

You feel so calm and relaxed now, so full of energy and strength. Resting on the ground you start to notice the warmth of the sun on your face and body. It feels so good, this golden light that warms you. And, as you relax and enjoy the feeling of the sun on your body, you find yourself feeling as if you yourself *are* the sun, you feel as if you are glowing with energy, radiant with light. Every cell of your body feels so vibrant – filled with warmth, vitality and power.

Stay with this feeling for as long as you like, and then gradually become aware of lying beside the lake again. Feel the earth beneath you, the clear water of the lake in front of you, the blue sky above you, and the sun shining down on you. Then slowly become aware of being in the here and now. Become aware of your body, stretch your fingers and toes, then open your eyes.

This visualization exercise can be very relaxing and healing, but you can make it even more effective by grounding the experience in your body, either by going for a walk, a swim or by having a massage – or, if you can arrange it, having a mud bath!

At the summer camps of the Order of Bards, Ovates and Druids, we always dig a mud bath, so that after such an exercise we can take off our clothes, wander out into the sun, and sink into warm invigorating mud. Many people, after they have had a mud bath, go into the sweathouse. Let's join Elidir again to hear more about this:

 # THE COLLOQUY (PART II)

'Just as the Native Americans work in sweat lodges,' Elidir explains, 'The Celts, and, undoubtedly, the ancient Druids too, discovered the healing power of combining water and fire as many cultures have done, and developed sweathouses. Piles of heated stones with traces of post holes have been found by archaeologists at a number of prehistoric sites in Britain, and up until the nineteenth century the Irish used sweathouses fuelled by peat, which they called *Tigh n'Alluis*. We have revived the practice here, and every week an experienced member holds a sweathouse ceremony over there,' she says, pointing to a domed structure that you learn is a bender made of hazel rods covered with tarpaulins.

'I shall not talk about it too much, because these ceremonies are sacred to us, and you need to understand what you are doing with them. Besides, there are health risks involved – if you have any kind of heart trouble, for instance. We dedicate the whole ceremony to the goddess Brighid, because she is the goddess of Healing. She is also the goddess of the holy well and the sacred flame – of water and fire – so it is fitting that a ceremony that uses the power of water and fire should be dedicated to her. Imagine how you would feel if, after your Blessing of the Elements meditation and mud-bath experience, you went through a sweathouse ceremony too.

'Having explained all this, you can see how fundamental Nwyfre is to our health and well-being. Imagine living close to the earth, in a simple wooden house, surrounded by gardens and like-minded folk. Now imagine that you are eating home-grown food, drinking lots of pure water, and allowing your body to feel sunlight and air, wind and rain without feeling you always have to be covered with clothes for the sake of so-called decency. Imagine that every so often you are having a mud bath and sweathouse ceremony, and that every autumn you undertake a three-day cleansing with apples.

'If you ever do get ill, there would be aromatherapists and healers nearby to massage you with herbs and oils, to treat you with elixirs, teas and poultices, and to listen to your problems – because often, as you know, our physical ills are caused by troubles of the heart and mind. That is why we need to train people to be Soul Friends – *Anam Caras* as they are called in Celtic spirituality – to act as counsellors, good listeners who know how to hear truly the voice of your soul, without letting themselves get in the way.

'Finally, let me tell you about the way in which celebrating the seasonal festivals can help you live long and stay healthy. Everyone wants a quick fix to get healthy, but in reality it takes a while and one reason that many people are unhealthy is because they have separated themselves from the rhythm of Nature. But if you celebrate the eight seasonal festivals, you are consciously connecting to the rhythm and the power of the seasons and the natural world. Over time their magic starts to work on you – you become attuned to the cycles of the Earth and this has a profound effect on your feelings of health and well-being.'

HISTORY

Until recently, most doctors and scientists laughed at the idea that a spiritual approach to healing was necessary. Their rational approach to medicine had brought enormous advances in their understanding and treatment of disease, and had swept away much superstition and ignorance. But they had also refused to give any consideration to the value of alternative methods of healing, particularly when these were based on a spiritual understanding of the human being. In the last few years, though, their approach has started to change. Little by little, scientific research into alternative medicine is starting to show that a wide range of these practices do actually work: acupuncture, herbalism (both Western and Oriental), osteopathy and aromatherapy, all of these alternative approaches have been found to be beneficial and are being increasingly recommended by orthodox doctors, and are being introduced into major hospitals.

But Druidcraft, like the Taoism of China, tells us that we can aim for more than just ways of repairing our bodies if they get ill. It tells us that we can strive for superior health and for rejuvenation, for youthfulness. In Celtic lands there are still Wells of Eternal Youth, where we are advised to bathe at dawn on Midsummer's morning, and the old tales inspire us with stories of *Tir n'an Og* – the Land of Eternal Youth. If we could unearth a recipe for Eternal Youth what would it tell us? What if our ancestors have given us the clues to creating vibrant health in the old stories and folk remedies that have been handed down to us from generation to generation?

Although we may not be able to find a complete recipe for rejuvenation, and although there are no records of an entire healing system that comes exclusively from the practices of the ancient Druids or the old Cunning Folk, the Witches, it is possible to research, practice and evolve healing methods that are compatible with, and even derive from, these sources. Recent findings, such as those given in Mary Beith's *Healing Threads – Traditional Medicines of the Highlands and Islands* show that today we can still trace valuable healing techniques back to the early Druids. The knowledge found within the herbal of the Welsh Physicians of Mydvai (published by The Welsh Manuscript Society, 1861) certainly derives from much earlier sources that could have originated in the Ovates or Witches of earlier days. This herbal, written in the thirteenth century, may contain material dating from as early as the sixth century – the time when Druidry was being superseded by Christianity. It is possible that as the door between one era and the next was closed, some of the ancients' knowledge managed to slip through.

Illness is ubiquitous and any method or remedy found to work is likely to be handed down through generations. Research biologist Dr Andrew Allen explains in his book, *A Dictionary of Sussex Folk Medicine* that the majority of country folk did not use professional medical treatment until the late nineteenth century. It was prohibitively expensive, often geographically distant, and frequently it did not work or was even downright dangerous. Instead, they relied on home treatment using traditional family remedies. Dr Allen goes on:

> *If home treatment failed, or if the ailment fell into specific categories, [they] might turn to a 'white Witch', 'wise woman', 'cunning woman' or 'cunning man', often skilled in herbal medicine, who might cure the ailment by prescribing a folk remedy, by therapeutic white magic, charms or spells (or the lifting of curses or spells inflicted by Witches). More often it was a melange of both.*

> *Such individuals, based in the local community, commonly claimed to have a 'gift' for healing, either acquired or inherited. They operated in the context of the local economy and seldom asked for money for their services, preferring to be paid, tangibly or intangibly, in kind. 'Cunning folk' of both sexes were reputedly once as common as the parish clergy, and to be found in every parish in the country.*

In England, there were still Cunning Folk in some villages as late as the 1930s, and some of their methods of treatment have been recorded and tested with modern science (such as those of Grandmother Huggett). For example, staunching wounds with cobwebs is sensible – the filaments contain blood-clotting proteins – but glow-worm wine has no apparent healing properties!

The lore has not all been lost. Like Miach's pattern on Airmid's cloak, it has been scattered, and it is up to us to combine the rigours of modern understanding with a respect for ancient knowledge, to create ways of healing that work for us in today's world.

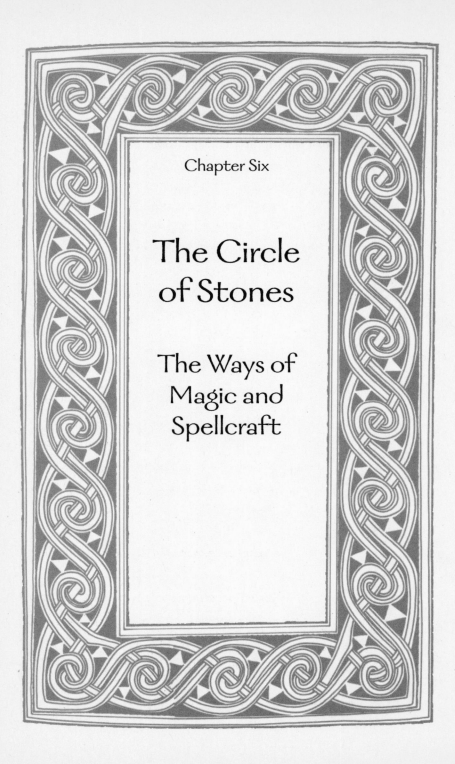

Chapter Six

The Circle of Stones

The Ways of Magic and Spellcraft

You have a Druid craft of wicked sound
Wrung from the cold women of the sea

W.B. Yeats

Adne, son of Uthider, of the tribes of Connaught, had the
greatest knowledge of wisdom and poetry in Ireland. He had
a son, Nede, who went to Scotland to learn from Eochu
Horsemouth, with whom he stayed until he learned great skill.

One day the youth went forth along the edge of the sea -
poets ever believed that the brink of water was a place of
revelation. And as he stood there, he heard a sound like a
wailing chant of sadness, which seemed strange to him. So he
cast a spell upon the water, causing it to reveal to him what
was the matter. And the wave declared that the wailing he
had heard was for the death of his father, Adne.

The Colloquy of the Two Sages, trans. John Matthews

Druidry, Wicca and Druidcraft are paths of magic, but with the use of magic comes responsibility. Here, in the quotation above from an old Irish text that describes a dialogue between two magicians – two Bardic shamans – we see Nede casting a spell of Questing Magic that seeks to determine the cause behind the world of appearances. Magic can indeed transcend the limitations of space and time, but it should only be attempted by those who are truly prepared for the knowledge they might acquire, and for the consequences of their actions.

THE BARD'S TALE

LUGAID THE FIRE MAKER

If you were to walk beside Loch Lugh-phorta, that brooding Loch that lies a few miles to the east of the Shannon as it snakes its way towards the sea past Ballina, you would find, in the meadow that slopes towards the southern edge of the loch, a low flat mound: an ancient barrow. And it is in this barrow that lies the body of Lugaid Delbaeth, the Druid that everyone feared, called 'The Fire Producer' because he could make fire with the power of his mind and the brilliance of his speech.

It was Lugaid who could also read fire like no other. He could gaze into flames of any kind – in a raging bonfire, a glowing hearth fire, or the sultry glimmer of a bedside candle. And he could speak of the future from what he saw. As two red-hot logs crumbled as one into a heap on the grate, he would foretell the fall of two great houses in a conflagration of hatred and war. As flames shot from the boughs of ancient ash, felled in the king's forest, he would speak of love born in the heat of summer, and of the king's issue who would ride triumphant to the court of Tara bringing honour and riches to his tribe and family.

If you go now to sit on the barrow of Lugaid the Fire Gazer, the Fire Maker, and look out at the Loch of Lugh-phorta, it might just happen that after a while you would fall into a sleep. In the old days this is exactly what the magician's apprentice would be told to do. The apprentice would have to sleep out on the old barrows, on the burial mounds of the heroes and heroines of the tribe, to seek a dream, to enter the world of the heroes, to be given guidance and courage, inspiration and insight into the world beyond time. And if you did this, if you fell asleep, you might find yourself encountering the ghostly form of Lugaid, who with right arm outstretched would create a raging fire out of nothing but the pointing of his finger towards the earth. And with a wistful, world-weary, but kindly smile, he would motion you to sit beside the fire with him, and he would begin to tell you the story of the land around you, and of the fate of his family of seven children:

'Our lives changed forever the day our daughter Deidre married that wretch Trad,' he would say, gazing into your eyes with an Otherworldly look of sorrow, which, even as you waited for his next words, would give way to a smile of the deepest wisdom.

'She loved him dearly, though, and in the end it is love that counts. And however hard your fate may seem, still it conceals a jewel, a hidden purpose – as we were about to discover.

'Trad had hardly a penny to his name, and just a few acres on the side of the hill that he tried to farm as best he could. But he was a man who loved to plough and sow in the warm embrace of his wife, rather than in the rough earth of a northern hillside. And so his family grew and grew. It seems as if no year passed without Deirdre giving birth to a new grandchild of mine, until, in desperation, Trad came to me one day and asked me to use my Druid powers to see how he might obtain more land to farm.

'How could I refuse my own son-in-law? He needed the land to feed his children – my grandchildren! I asked him to make his offerings to the goddess – to Brighid of the Flame and of the Waters. At dawn the next day, he cast coins of gold and silver into her well, uttering the Prayers of Wishing, before making his way to my forest hermitage. This was where I did my magic, consulted the oracles, and journeyed to the Otherworld. This was a place I had built with my own hands, apart from the hubbub of the family, from the wrangling and tussling of my six sons – and the attentions of my three wives!

'When Trad arrived I bad him sit beside my altar. I called to the gods of Sea, Sky and Land. I called to Brighid to bring her flame to my aid, and when I felt her power surge through me, I flung my arm out and with a cry pointed to the centre of my altar. And there sprang up at once a roaring flame. Gazing directly into its heart, as I had been taught to do so long ago by my Master, I entered – almost in an instant – the trance state of *imbas*. Now the power of the Goddess flowed through me – not as fire, but as Inspiration. And opening my mouth to let Her speak through me, I turned to Trad and cried out, "This know today. Ask of any man to surrender his land, and your command he will be honour bound to obey!"

'The flame died down and extinguished itself on my altar. The imbas had flowed and was gone from me. I collapsed beside the altar, breathing deeply, thanking the Goddess, waiting for my strength to return. When I could stand again, I turned to face Trad. But there was an evil gleam in his eye, as he stared at me with a look of defiance saying, "On this day of mine, I ask that you, Lugaid, surrender your lands to me!" And so, in an instant, my destiny was changed forever. I was honour bound to hand my estate at once to Trad.

'What thoughts raged through my head! Although my heart swelled to think that my daughter and grandchildren would be well-provided for by my bounteous fields and forests, I knew that Trad would scarcely tend these lands with the care they needed. And why did he not ask another man to surrender his land, rather than his own father-in-law? What would I do with my six sons and three wives? Where would we go? Where would we farm and grow old? But I trusted in the Goddess. I had seen enough of life to know that however bleak the future seems, still in the darkness She is present, guiding us with Her hand.

'Within days Trad had revealed his true colours. Despite the protestations of our daughter and our grandchildren, he ordered us to leave. With cruel eyes and vicious words he cast us from our house. I will never forgot the look of horror on the face of my daughter, and the cries of anguish from her children, as the cart carrying our family and its few possessions trundled away from the homestead towards the river.

'We crossed the Shannon at Ballina and headed east towards the hills and Carn Fiacha. We reached the lakeside at dusk, and as we stood gazing on its waters, three swans rose from the surface of the lake. They circled thrice above the lake, and then flew west towards the setting sun. And it was then I knew that this would be the place of my growing old and my death. It was a place of great beauty and stillness, and I saw now why the Goddess had led us here. My wives knew this for themselves too, and since no one had claimed these lands, we set about building our home and tilling the soil. But all along we knew that our sons needed to find their own lands to farm, and one morning at dawn my spirit guides woke me with the thought ringing in my head that I must light a great fire, and pray to Brighid to find land for my sons.

'All that day we gathered wood from far and wide, until by night-fall we had built the greatest bonfire I had ever seen. The ten of us stood in a circle around the fire. We called to the spirits of East, West, South and North. We called to the Four Winds. We called to the spirits of Mountain and Plain, of River, Lake and Sea. And then I called to Brighid and once more Her power surged through me, and I was able to fling my arm out and, with the Incantation of Fire on my lips, point to the centre of the woodpile. All at once, flames of red, green, blue and gold sprang from its heart, and it was as if every fire sprite in Erin was dancing in its midst. I called then to Brighid that we might be shown new lands for our sons, and in that moment the entire pile burst into a mighty blaze, and five streams of fire shot forth and ran like molten lava along the ground to the far horizons.

'In the wild beauty of this moment, there came a stillness within my heart. And in this stillness I seemed to hear the voice of a woman, who, in deep and sonorous tones, spoke to me saying, "Hold Nos, your youngest son, close to you. He must stay with you here till you die. But send your five older sons to follow each one of them a different stream. Where each stream ends there should each one settle. And just as the Sacred Well feeds the five streams of life-giving water that flow across Tir n'an Og, so will your fire become the hearth fire of the tribe that will grow from the seed of your children. And from all five directions they will come to gather at this hearth fire at the times of celebration – Bealteinne and Lughnasadh, Samhain and Imbolc.'

And as you hear this, the figure of Lugaid seated beside the fire, talking to you of his life and lands, of the story of the origin of his tribe and their country, slowly begins to fade until you find yourself waking up on the low flat grassy mound beside Loch Lugh-phorta, with the sun rising in the east, as three white swans come to land on the still waters of the lake.

THE COLLOQUY

Awakening from the reverie induced by the Bard's tale, as if from a dream, you make your way with your fellow students towards the ancient stone circle that stands upon the hillside above the houses and fields of Avronelle, until at last you see your teacher, Elidir, gazing out to sea.

On hearing your approach she turns towards you and invites you to sit beside her on the grass outside the circle.

'Let us talk about magic,' she begins. 'People tend to think that magic is one thing, when in reality it is a number of things. As followers of this way, our aim is to lead magical lives – to experience life as magical. You have seen we do many things to encourage this. We perform ceremonies eight times a year to attune ourselves to the magic of the seasons, we take magical journeys in consciousness to explore the Otherworld, we enact Rites of Passage to mark important moments in our lives, and we connect to the magical current of Nwyfre to bring energy and vitality to our lives.

'You see, life is fundamentally magical, and to experience its magic we simply have to get in tune with it and then the magic just flows through us. And when this happens, when you get in tune with the flow of life, synchronicity occurs more often. You meet the right person at the right time, you open a book at just the right place to receive the guidance you need, you get offered the job just when you need it.

'That is one way of looking at magic – seeing it all around you in Nature, and opening yourself to it with this way of living. But there are also other kinds of magic. The most obvious kind that everyone knows about is Stage Magic.

'Good stage magicians keep surprising you. They show you that you can't rely on your senses. They play with your sense of reality until you don't know what is real and what is illusion. Their goal is to entertain and amuse you, by showing illusion after illusion, and this delights you because they reveal the limitations of your senses and your mind.

'But that is as far as it goes. There is a connection with what we do on this way in as much as we are trying to go beyond the illusions generated by the mind, but that's about it. So, leaving aside Stage Magic, there are only two types of magic we are interested in – Practical and Alchemical.

'Alchemical Magic involves working on yourself. It is called alchemical because in alchemy the idea is to change "base metal" into gold, the ordinary into the extraordinary. Our goal is to do this with our own lives, our own selves. That is much of the purpose of following a path such as Druidcraft. At each stage we are developing ourselves, our capacities, our abilities, our powers, so that gradually we are growing, evolving and transforming as human beings. You could use a less evocative term, such as "the magic of personal or spiritual development", but alchemy conveys the power that this way of working has to provoke profound changes and gradual transformations.

'The idea in alchemy is that you start off with the "base metal" that is equivalent to all the raw material that you possess as a personality and a soul. Then, by following a spiritual path, you gradually transform this into a quality of being which literally radiates. That is why people who are on this path often have a quality of youthfulness and life which is almost tangible. And, in accordance with the Law of the Returning Tide, if you start to radiate positive energy out into the world, it will start to flow back into your life in all sorts of ways.

'People who are clairvoyant or who have a sixth sense can see or feel this in people. Some people's auras are grey and the energy they radiate is minimal, other people's auras literally shine and the energy they radiate is strong and positive, so they naturally attract people and circumstances around them that respond to this energy.

'All the techniques and ideas described in our discussions can be used for the purposes of Alchemical Magic – the visualizations, the ceremonies, the mud baths and sweathouse ceremonies, they are all designed to help us become radiant, to help us grow spiritually, and to help us stay physically and psychologically healthy.

'In addition to this way of working, there is another kind of magic – Practical Magic. But before you start studying this, it is important to know why you are interested in magic, and what you would do with any magical skills or knowledge you might obtain.' Elidir motions Brendan to step forward. He seats himself beside her, and they begin their colloquy.

'Why are you interested in magic?' asks Elidir.

'Because I know there is so much more to life than meets the eye,' replies Brendan. 'Behind the world of appearances, I know there are all sorts of influences operating, and I would love to know what they are and how I can work with them to enhance my life and other people's.'

'Yes, but what would you specifically like to do if you became a magician?' asks Elidir, gazing at him intently.

Brendan replies, 'I'd like to be able to travel into the Otherworld to meet otherworldly beings – people who have died or who are not yet born, and animal spirits, and those beings they call Fairies and Devas. I'm not even sure if these all exist, so I'd like to find that out too.'

'But why would you want to do that – apart from curiosity?' asks Elidir, raising her eyebrows in a questioning look.

'I'd like to hear their wisdom,' answers Brendan. 'I'd like to ask them for guidance for my life, and for how we can help solve the world's problems. And, of course, I'd be fascinated to explore their worlds and to learn about how they live.'

'Are there any other things you would like to do?' asks Elidir.

Brendan replies, 'Well, I'd like to be able to do magic to help people and to influence positively certain things, but I'm a bit wary of this kind of magic because when people talk about it, it often seems like meddling to me.'

'I agree, but let's look at this in more detail,' says Elidir who takes her staff and uses it to draw a symbol on the earth. It is a Celtic triple knot. She then turns to Brendan and says, 'In Druidcraft we divide Practical Magic into three kinds: Questing, Changing and Making. They each have very different purposes, but there is some overlap – hence the symbol that we use.'

'Broadly, there are three reasons for doing magic. One is for research – getting information, finding answers to questions. We use Questing Magic for this. Another is for effecting transformation – encouraging certain outcomes, changing things for the better. We use Changing Magic for this. And the third reason we do magic is for manifestation, which involves bringing something to birth in the world. We use the Magic of Making for this.'

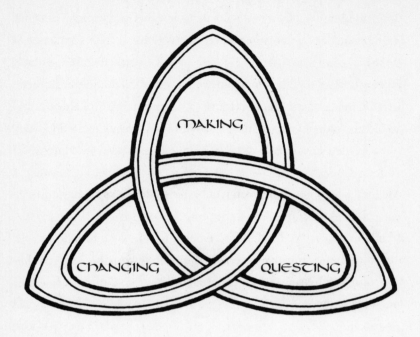

THE MAGIC OF QUESTING

'Let us begin with research. That was the first reason you gave for wanting to do magic – you wanted to learn about the Otherworld. This is what attracts many people to the subject of magic. They have heard about astral travel, or maybe past-life regression, and they want to explore their previous lives on Earth, or they want to meet their totem animals or talk to beings from other planets or to angels and fairies. This is a very important area for study, one that science is only just beginning to explore. But the magical traditions have been using their own techniques to explore this field for years, using divination, journeying, shape shifting, past-life recall and future-life exploration, to get data, ideas, inspiration and insight.

'In divination we take a tool such as tarot cards or astrology to try to peer beyond the veil of appearances, to look deeper into the causes of things. We can also use the tree language of Ogham or totem animals as an oracle, or we can take a journey into the Otherworld. For this we use a magical ceremony to create the appropriate atmosphere and attract the right energies for the enterprise, and then we use the power of music and the human voice to carry our consciousness into other realms. In reality, this way of working is shamanism, because a shaman is someone who journeys, who goes into a trance or altered states to obtain information for healing or guidance.

'So, when someone wants to use magic for their research, when they want to undertake a Quest into the Otherworld, they decide which tool they will use to do this – divination or journeying – then they use one or more aids, such as ritual, music, dance or another person's voice, to help them on their quest. With these aids they can then steer themselves towards the exploration of either the past or future, or towards meeting spirit animals or beings in the Otherworld.

'There are also more esoteric methods, such as rolling you up in a bull's hide and sending you to sleep by a waterfall. That was a way the Irish Druids sometimes determined the next king in ancient times. They used that magic to send their Druid-shaman into the Otherworld to get the information they needed.'

'Why wrapping in a hide, and why the waterfall?' asks Brendan.

'You could explain it by saying that the strange physical sensation of being tightly rolled up, and of your brain being bombarded by the roar of the waterfall, created a powerful state of altered consciousness,' replies Elidir. 'But that is just part of the reason – an explanation of the fuel used to project the Druid into the Otherworld. The real skill lay in the Druid-shaman knowing where to go in that Otherworld, and who to ask for advice once he was there.'

Elidir falls silent for a while, looking out to sea and then at the stone circle. After a moment she invites you all to enter the circle of stones. As you follow her, you notice that she pauses at the entrance to the circle in the West, touching the gateway stones each side of her lightly, before stepping through.

As you step forward into the circle, straight away you feel a change in the atmosphere. There is a deep, strong feeling here, as if you are in the presence of Greater Powers. Elidir motions you all to the northern side of the circle, then sits down in front of a stone, and continues:

THE MAGIC OF MAKING

'The Druids of old discovered a very special kind of magic – how to make objects appear out of thin air!' she announces dramatically.

'And this is the sort of thing they produced.' She opens her hand to produce an old Celtic buckle, made out of silver with delicate knot-work curling around every part of it. You look at her puzzled. Is she suggesting that they literally conjured such things out of nothing?

'First they captured the idea, they received the inspiration to make such a thing. They might even have done some Questing Magic to do this and been given the design by a guardian spirit in the Otherworld,' says Elidir. 'Then they nurtured and developed it in the cauldron of their minds and hearts. Then, at exactly the right time and in exactly the right way, they gave birth to it in the forge.'

'So they didn't just make it appear literally out of thin air,' says Brendan.

'They did,' insists Elidir. 'It wasn't an instant process, that is all. When you have an idea for making or doing something, it starts in "thin air" – as an intangible thought. But a day, a month or a year later, there is the meal, the building, the painting. The magic of making is the magic of creation itself.'

'But what is so special about that? People are creating things all the time,' Brendan responds.

'You are right. But there is more to it than that,' replies Elidir. 'Certainly, the three activities of Questing, Making and Changing occur all the time. People are researching, creating things and influencing events every day. Magic is no different in that sense. But what is different about it is that with magic we are working in the inner world. We are not just working in the outside world of effects, but going to a deeper, more causal level, where ultimately we can have more effect.

'Once you understand the concept of the web – of the way everything is connected – it means you can literally "work the web" to magical effect. It is as if there is an invisible pattern of connections between all things. Most people don't know about these, and they try to make or influence things on the surface, while the magician goes quietly into a magic circle, contacts the web, and then sends impulses or messages down the right filaments to produce the required effect.

'The first magic to learn in Druidcraft is the Magic of Making. It is the magic of the Bard, the magic of creativity – of singing, music making, storytelling, painting, writing, acting, sculpting and dancing. Of course, you can do all these things without knowing anything about magic, but if you do know about it, you can be even more creative.

'You can take the whole creative process and apply magic to each of its stages. The first stage in making something, manifesting something in the world, is getting the idea, the inspiration. What is it that you want to create? Often we get plenty of ideas, but the art is in getting the right idea – right ethically and right in the sense of it being a good idea that needs to be born into the world.

'To help us do this, our magic is so broad that you cannot confine it to one technique. It involves developing our consciousness, our selves as vessels, as receptors that can capture the best ideas. Think of those great radio telescope dishes that can capture radio signals from distant stars. Gradually, through our development as spiritual and human beings, we can become like those great dishes, picking up distant signals.'

'Where do they come from?' asks Brendan.

'Who do they come from, is a better question,' replies Elidir. 'Perhaps we can capture signals – ideas and inspiration – from advanced beings on other planets, from angels, from wise souls who now live in other dimensions or in physical bodies on the other side of the world. Perhaps they originate deep in our own subconscious, perhaps they float like clouds in the collective unconscious of humanity, perhaps they are beamed to us by unimaginably advanced intelligences far away. Wherever they come from, we believe that the more we meditate and live our lives in tune with Nature and with Spirit, the more likely we are to receive these messages and ideas.

'The way we live prepares us magically for inspiration, which is called Awen in Druidry. Awen is Welsh for "gift of the gods", "blessings of the gods" or, simply, "inspiration". It was Awen that the goddess Ceridwen brewed in her cauldron. We can chant for Awen in our ceremonies, and we can also use a technique that was used by bards in Scotland right up until the seventeenth century. They used to cultivate inspiration by going into dark bothies – cottages – closing all the windows, and lying on a bed with a scarf tied round their eyes. They did this so there was no light disturbing them and, of course, it was completely silent up there in the wilds of the Highlands. Sometimes they put a stone on their chests too. They were doing this to create a type of sensory deprivation. Present-day researchers have found that people can have all sorts of extrasensory experiences under these conditions. So, you can see that the Bard-shamans were using these techniques to travel into the Otherworld to get their inspiration, their information. That is the overlap between the different types of magic that I mentioned when I showed you the triple knot. They are using Questing Magic for the initial stages of Making Magic.'

'I can see how you are seeking inspiration in all these different ways, but once you've got it, what do you do next?' asks Brendan.

'You are trying to make a dream come true,' says Elidir. 'Once you receive the inspiration you have to nurse the baby that is growing inside. Making Magic is no different to bringing a child into the world, or planting a seed and tending the seedling that grows from that seed. Your dream, your desire or goal is the seed. Do nothing with it and it will die.

'You need to nurse the dream, so don't try to give birth to it too fast. Dreams need nurturing with rumination, with daydreaming around them. They even need ignoring for a while, so they can grow and incubate in darkness. Don't keep digging the seed up to see how it's doing. Focus on something else while feeling happy and confident that the seed is germinating – drink in art and music, poetry and song. Walk in the woods, talk with friends, enjoy being alive.

'When the time comes to nourish the seed with thought, go at it sideways. Make a collage of photos, drawings and poems about it. Make an altar or sacred place in your house or garden with objects and images that relate to it. Read books about it. Be open to new ideas and feelings about it. Get friends to play devil's advocate. Argue passionately for it and passionately against it. Be prepared to lose the dream and find another. Not every child gets to be born. Don't think you are always right or that you always know what is best for you or for the world. But, after all this, if your passion is still there and you want to make it happen, take the next step.

'You see, the art of this kind of magic – Making Magic – is completely natural,' continues Elidir. 'It is a Magic that follows the same sequence or stages that making a baby follows – first you conceive, then you gestate, then you give birth, then you take care of the newborn baby before you let it go out into the world. And all the disasters that can befall a physical pregnancy can also happen to this kind of spiritual or creative pregnancy – you can miscarry at any time, or have a stillbirth.

'Often people get ideas which they give birth to prematurely, and so the project withers and dies because it is not strong enough to survive in the outside world. They should have kept it inside, in their heart and imagination for a little longer – thought it through more, allowed it to develop more.

'The art in this kind of magic is the art of parenting, of learning how to mother and father the idea into the world. You need to develop your nurturing, protective, supporting and containing abilities, and to harness all of these in the service of manifesting your idea in the world. It is all about learning how to use the chalice and the wand. The wand represents the masculine principle of focus and direction, and the chalice represents the feminine principle of containing and nurturing. Together they bring life and creativity into the world.'

'The God and the Goddess again?' says Brendan.

'Exactly,' replies Elidir. 'Wiccans realize this by having the High Priestess plunge a dagger into a chalice at the high point of their ceremonies. This symbolizes the union of the masculine and feminine principles, the union of God and Goddess that creates the world. It is the same thing in our own worlds too; it is the union of our ability to direct and focus our intentions, with our ability to nurture and contain them. Whether or not we can successfully unite these two abilities determines whether we can bring ideas to birth in the world.

'Some people can only wave their wands around, focusing and controlling but never achieving much of deep value. Others can be supportive and nurturing but lacking in any focus themselves. The magician manages to unite these two abilities within themselves to be creative in the world.'

After a pause, Brendan says, 'Tell me about the third kind of magic, the magic that tries to change things.'

THE MAGIC OF CHANGING

Elidir looks around the circle of stones and then far off into the distance, before turning to Brendan again and saying, 'Most people feel at the mercy of circumstances. The world is just too unpredictable, too big, and there are too many people and too much power being wielded for them to feel as if they are in charge of their lives. But magic says that the world you see is the result of hidden forces and influences that you can learn to understand and change. You can learn how to go behind the scenes, symbolically, and open a window to let in more air and light.'

'But isn't that dangerous?' asks Brendan.

'Why is it any more dangerous than being a helpless victim in a world of effects?' counters Elidir.

'Because then at least you are innocent. As soon as you start meddling with "hidden influences" you run the risk of doing the wrong thing,' replies Brendan.

'You are right,' says Elidir, 'which is why with the Magic of Changing you have to be very careful. You must be fully aware of the Law of the Returning Tide, and you must understand how to work the magic in just the right way. It is not for beginners. You need to have worked with the other two kinds of magic first – experiencing the Otherworld in journeying, and working with each of the stages of the Magic of Making, learning how to receive Awen and help it manifest in the world. Only then are you ready to work with the type of magic that involves generating influences in the world.

'So, although I cannot train you fully in this last kind of magic yet, I can at least tell you a little about it.' Elidir gestures to the stones around you, 'A stone circle is like an electrical accumulator. It can store and release energy, and that is why it is a good place to work with the Magic of Changing. The primary tool for this kind of magic is the spell and this usually takes the form of a magical chant expressing an intention or desire. So, we perform a ceremony at the centre of which is a spell. We dance round and round chanting this spell and, as we do so, the energy in the circle builds and builds, and the stones add to the effect, helping to store and increase the effectiveness of the charge, just as an accumulator does with electricity. As we reach the peak of intensity, we all drop down to the ground – usually with exhaustion – and as we do this, we let go of all thoughts and desires, just knowing and trusting that the spell will work, carried by the energy generated by us and intensified by the stone circle.

'If you're on your own it's a bit harder to build up the energy, but you can still do it by vizualizing your intention strongly and by focusing on the power flowing through the words of the spell. And you can dance on your own as well if you like.'

'But what is a spell?' asks Brendan.

'A spell is simply a wish expressed in a magical way. A spell asks for healing or blessing, or for something concrete and specific, such as a new house or job. Unfortunately, it can also be used to ask for something unpleasant, as in a curse, which is also a wish, but a destructive one.

'Obviously, performing spells to harm or curse is out of the question – once you truly understand the Law of the Returning Tide you will know that. But using spellcraft for what appear to be good ends can also create problems and, unless you get it exactly right, the results can be disastrous. Most people think that all they have to do is make sure their spells are for good things, but it is not as simple as that. Sometimes we don't know what is good for us, or what making our wish come true might entail.

'I know of someone who cast a spell to get more time in her busy life. It worked – she was fired a few days afterwards and found herself with all the time in the world, but with no money. And I have heard of a woman who worked a spell to get a million dollars. This succeeded too – a few days later her husband fell down a lift shaft. His life was insured for a million dollars and his wife received the money only weeks after she performed the spell.

'So, just asking for what you want can be a risky business. The trouble with teaching spell-making to novices is that they want to get started straight away on doing spells to get all the things they think they need – boyfriends or girlfriends, cars, jobs and money. It becomes a sort of spiritual consumerism and it is coming from a place of lack – or perceived lack. That is not a good place from which to base your magical intention because, according to the Law of Resonance, if you believe you are lacking in something, you will attract more of that sense of lack into your life. In the first example I just gave, the spellcaster swapped a sense of a lack of time for a lack of money. In the second story, the woman swapped a lack of money for the lack of her husband.

'Instead of working in this way, you need to approach spell-making from a position of trust and confidence that everything is working out more perfectly than you could imagine, and that you are using your prayers and spells to align yourself more fully with the current of abundance and rightness that flows through life. That is also how the best healing works – you realign yourself with the healing and beneficent current of life.

'But how do you work a spell?' asks Brendan. 'I'm still not sure exactly what a spell is and how you make it!'

'A spell is just the expression of a wish, desire or intention expressed in such a way that you believe or hope it will come true,' replies Elidir. 'So really it is like a prayer, where you are petitioning a Higher Power. But the magical techniques used with a spell can make it more effective than prayer.'

WISHES, PRAYERS AND SPELLS

'Let's now look at wishes, prayers and spells, and see how they are related – and how they are each somehow different too. In the days of the ancient Druids, they would often cast spells by throwing precious objects into sacred lakes or wells. We still act out this custom, in a watered-down way, when we come across a wishing well. We throw a coin into the well and ask for what we want. It is an example of an ancient custom that still exists today, even if most people don't know of its true origins. In the old days this was a magical act, whereas today we make a wish without necessarily believing in the likelihood that it will come true. That is a wish – you just say it or think it without any special technique or belief that it will happen.

'Now, a prayer is also a wish, but you actually ask a Higher Power, such as God or the Goddess, for your wish to come true: "*O Goddess, may there be peace on Earth!*" is an example of a short prayer, whereas a wish would simply be "*I wish there was peace on Earth.*" To turn a prayer into a spell you would need to add a further step, such as saying it nine times as you strike a bell, visualizing waves of peace rippling outwards.

'A spell takes the desire that could be expressed in a wish or prayer, and uses the power of ceremony, the power of the words that are used, the power of incantation or chanting, and sometimes dancing as well, and combines all this with the power of visualization. So you can see that it is more complicated, but it can also be much more effective.

'In addition, spell-makers can perform their work at particular phases of the moon or times of the year to take advantage of the natural tides or energies that are flowing in the world, such as the tides of sowing and growing, reaping, dying and renewal that you have already learned about. Some people also use astrology to determine exactly the right time to work a particular spell.

'A spell works with the power of the voice, ideally sung, chanted or spoken with great feeling. And it works with the spell-maker's ability to visualize strongly the desired outcome. A skilled magician can simply chant a spell, powerfully visualizing its realization in the world, and that will be sufficient. Sometimes, the magician will also make a physical object to enhance the effect of the spell. She or he might write the spell down as they chant it on a special piece of parchment. Then they might burn it ritually to send its message out into the world, bury it in the ground, let the wind take it away or they might throw it into a stream – in each case using the power of one of the Four Elements. They might keep the piece of parchment and turn it into a charm, folding it up and putting it in a locket or sewing it into a garment. This is really based on the same idea as "clooties", which are little ribbons or rags that people in Cornwall and Ireland, in particular, tie on to trees around sacred wells after saying their prayers – making their wishes by the well. They work on exactly the same principle and the interesting thing is that you see this all over the world. In Native American sweat lodges they sometimes make prayer bundles of pinches of tobacco tied round with ribbon, and attach these to the framework of the lodge. In India and Tibet they make prayer flags, and tie ribbons to trees.

'The idea is that the physical object you make as you recite the spell or prayer then becomes charged with the vibration of your intent, and continues to emit that vibration long after you have finished the spell-making rite. You can also do this with crystals and stones, but it is vital that you don't get preoccupied with the physical object – the charm. Most people who start working with spells get so concerned with calculating the most propitious time to do them, and then with preparing the rite and the charm that will be made, that they don't have much energy left for formulating the words of the spell and visualizing it powerfully as they chant it. And they can be very short-sighted. They will do a spell to get a lover, for example, and forget to add the vital idea that whatever they ask for should be "for the greater good of all". And so the lover appears, but makes their life a misery.

'Asking for a specific type of person or physical object to come into your life can be disastrous. It's far better to ask for the essence of what you need – love, rather than a lover, for example. This gives life the opportunity to provide what you need in the best possible way, rather than in the way that you, with your limited viewpoint, have envisaged.

'Unfortunately, people are often drawn to magic because they want to use it only for themselves. But when you truly know yourself, you discover that the greatest happiness and fulfilment comes not only when your own needs are satisfied, but when you are also concerned with serving something more than yourself, when you are making a positive contribution to the world.

'If you approach the subject with superstition or selfish motives, you will become enmeshed in fear and fantasy, and the danger is that you may try to use magic to manipulate others.

'This is not to say that you cannot use spells for your own needs, but the best way to do this is not to ask for anything specific, but instead to use a spell to ask for positive qualities or to reinforce those qualities within yourself which will then, through resonance, bring you what you need. As an example, this version of St Patrick's Lorica – you may know it as St Patrick's Breastplate – which was developed from a pre-Christian invocation, is ideal as a spell spoken immediately on waking up, for protection or for overcoming feelings of weakness and vulnerability:

'I arise today through the strength of heaven: light of sun,
radiance of moon, splendour of fire, speed of lightning,
swiftness of wind, depth of sea, stability of earth, firmness
of rock!

Elidir then stands up and says, 'Let's work with these ideas now. I have been speaking to you about the way Druidcraft involves consciously sowing seeds for ourselves and for others. Come with me now and we will do this – we will perform a spell together!'

With that, you follow her as she leads you out of the circle, across the meadow and down towards the sea. The sun is setting now, its golden beams shining across the ocean in ribbons of liquid light. As you reach the shore, the sun finally sinks below the horizon, and the sky grows darker.

'Think of three gifts,' Elidir says softly to you all. 'One that you would like to receive in your life, one that you would like for those around you, and one that you would like for the world.'

As you think of each gift, you remember her words of caution and try to reach to the heart of what it is that you want – not just the exterior wish. And as you do this, Elidir is busy folding waxed paper. In fact, she is making six paper boats, and into each she places a small candle. 'Just watch me, and then when you are ready, do the same. Remember, it is the spirit in which you do this, the magical intent, that is important. The outer form is just the vehicle for the magic of your spell.' And so saying, she walks to the shoreline, raises her hands to the first stars of evening and calls out:

'O Goddess of the Earth and Heavens, God of the Moon and Stars, Creatures and Beings of all Realms, Spirits of Earth, Air, Fire and Water, Spirits of the Land and of the Sea, hear our prayers!'

Elidir then lights the candle of one boat and launches it carefully on the outgoing tide. As she does this, you hear her saying, more quietly now:

For myself, O Goddess, compassion and wisdom!'

Launching her second boat, she says:

'For those around me, good health and joy!'

And with her third boat:

'For all Beings, may Peace prevail on Earth!'

Gazing for a while as each tiny boat slowly drifts away, she then turns to you with a smile, and you step forward to launch your boats onto the sea of Dreams.

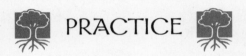

PRACTICE

Try the exercise suggested above, asking what it is you would truly like in each of the three realms – your own personal life, your immediate environment of friends, family and neighbourhood, and, finally, the wider world. The very act of determining these wishes should prove enlightening. Try to get to the root of each wish, so that, for example, if your wish is for protection from an aggressive person, go deeper to what you really want, which is the feeling of safety, and ask for that. Likewise with the desire for a physical object – if you want a car, what you really want is mobility, and behind that perhaps is the desire for freedom. The deeper you go, the closer you reach to the heart of your wish, the more effective will be your spell. If your wish is not for an obviously beneficent quality such as compassion, but for something more specific, always add a rider to your request, such as 'if it is in my best interests' or 'if it be for the greater good of all'.

Casting your spell across the water in a paper boat is based on an ancient custom, but this may be impractical for you. Instead, you could burn it in a candle flame, cast it to the wind on a feather or say it at a place that is special to you.

HISTORY

Spells and magic are integral to both Druidry and Witchcraft, although modern-day Druids are very cautious about working with Spellcraft. Most Druid groups either omit training in it or they teach it at a much later stage than their counterparts in Wicca. That is why people who only learn a little about modern Druidry do not find any mention of spells.

The ancient Druids were certainly involved in spellcraft – we know this from references to Druids' spells in the old texts. James Joyce says, 'The Gaelic word for Druidical is almost always applied where we should use the word magical – to spells, incantations, metamorphoses, etc.' and the Irish accounts, in particular, are full of references to Druidical charms, spells and magic.

Water was seen as an ideal medium for conveying spells, prayers and wishes, hence the use of the holy well and its derivative, the modern wishing well. Rivers and the sea were also considered to be directly connected to the Gods and the Otherworld. Druidry is of Indo-European origin, with many linguistic and cultural parallels being found between the two poles of Indo-European influence – Ireland and India. In India, at certain times, prayers are conveyed on light-boats. In describing a similar rite, performed by her Druid group, the author and herbalist Ellen Evert Hopman, writes, 'We added St. John's Wort to our candle boats. The ancients considered it the perfect combination of fire and water (and the whole universe is made of fire and water in Indo-European thinking). So it seemed right to use it in a ritual that involved putting sacred fire onto sacred water. It all goes back to the Agni/Soma hymns that are in the Rig Veda. The Rig Veda has proto-Indo-European roots, just like the Celtic tradition. Where fire and water come together one has the strongest possibility for magic. That is why a Fire Goddess like Brighid is invoked into a healing well.'

It is well known that Witches dance in a circle to create a 'cone of power' with which to project their spells. Dancing in a sacred circle is also carried out by Druids, and Charles Mackay suggests that hints of this, and traces of old Druidic chants, can be found in folk songs. He mentions an unusual word 'Rumbelow' which was used as a chorus in many old songs, both English and Scottish, as in 'With heigh and howe, and rumbelow'. In one old English sea shanty, recorded in 1609, the phrase 'dance the rumbelow' is translated as:

> Shall we go dance to round, around,
> Shall we go dance the round

He suggests that the word is 'apparently another remnant of the old Druidical chants sung by the priests when they walked in procession round their sacred circles of Stonehenge and others, and clearly traceable to the Gaelic – *riomball*, a circle; *riomballach*, circuitous; *riomballachd*, circularity'. Gerald Gardner also wrote, in *Witchcraft Today*,

'I fancy that certain practices, such as the use of the circle to keep the power in, were local inventions, derived from the use of the Druid or pre-Druid circle.'

In *The Book of Druidry*, Ross Nichols writes, 'Druidry is the Western form of an ancient universal philosophy, culture or religion, dating from the days of early man when the three were one. It is of the stone circle culture, the groves of sacred trees, the circular dance.' He also talks of the basic ideas of Witchcraft, including the cone of power generated by the ring dance in a stone circle, saying that Witchcraft knows a great deal about this, and that 'Druidry included these amongst its ideas, together with orientation and the later knowledge of sun and moon power.'

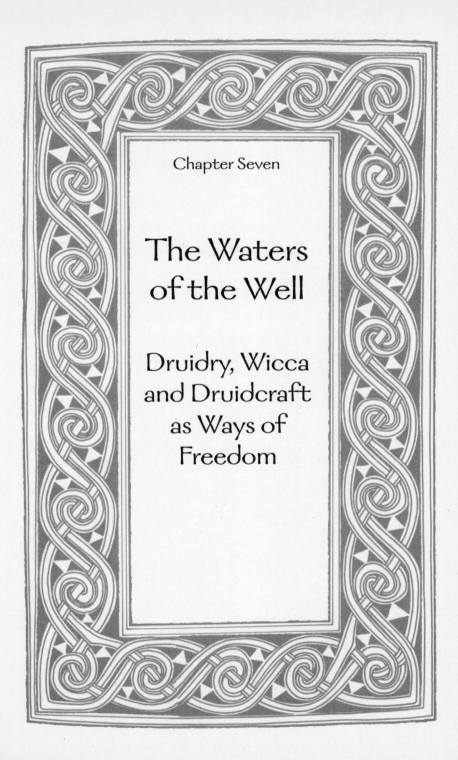

Chapter Seven

The Waters of the Well

Druidry, Wicca and Druidcraft as Ways of Freedom

I come from the West into the East
I am from the place of recollecting and my heart
is strangely stirred

On my right hand is the place of fire
and at my left hand is water
For my right hand holds the sun my father
and my left hand the moon my mother

Before me are the diamonds of light ...

'A Human Situation', Ross Nichols

It is time to leave Avronelle now. The sun has set. The candle-boats can no longer be seen. Fire and water have merged in the darkness of the ocean and a thousand stars have appeared in the night sky.

As you travel in your imagination away from Avronelle and back to the everyday world, you review your experiences in the Forest School. There you learnt about magic and spellcraft, seasonal rites and tides. You learned different rites: for initiation and home-blessing, for inner union, and for the blessings of the Goddess. You learned of healing and of herbs, and you listened to the old tales.

All that you learnt has been drawn from the world of inspiration – from the Otherworld and from the past – from images, ideas, stories, customs and folk practices of ancient times. And this has all been woven into a particular form and presented to you in the twenty-first century. Witchcraft and Druidry as they are practised today are also forms woven creatively in modern times, but they are forms drawing on the deepest roots of our spiritual ancestry. Druidcraft, Druidry and Wicca are above all spiritualities that foster creativity and freedom, and each of us is free to draw on these same inspirations to craft spiritual ways that suit us – in our circumstances, in our times.

Until recently, most people felt they had to make a choice between being a Witch or a Druid. You went for instinct or intellect, body or spirit – ecstatic dancing naked around a bonfire, or solemn ceremony in robed splendour amidst ancient stones. That distinction was real for many people, but it was fundamentally artificial, based on what people thought Witches and Druids were or should be.

In reality, both Druidry and Wicca draw upon the same wellspring of the Western Magical tradition for their style of working: in a magic circle that is often consecrated with fire and water, and where the four directions are invoked. They both rely heavily on the concept of four elements of Earth, Water, Air and Fire, with a fifth being Spirit. Both have a system of three degrees with three initiations. Both celebrate the eightfold year. But when they were developed in modern times, these virtually identical structures were first used in two entirely different ways. Wicca worked with the power of the union of opposites. Coven work was intense, private and dealt with the Gods. Druidry worked with the results of this union in creativity, and was less intense, often public, and dealt not so much with the Gods, as with the fruit of their inspiration in poetry and story. Both ways of working are powerful and valid, but there is no reason why they cannot be combined, and this is what has often happened amongst Druid and Wiccan groups in recent years.

At the heart of Wicca lies the theme of God and Goddess united as one. The introduction of this theme in modern times was inspired. It restored to indigenous, pagan spirituality the fundamental understanding of the importance of the relationship between the two great manifestations of divinity, which we call Masculine and Feminine. This understanding has a noble lineage, reaching its greatest sophistication in the Taoist and Tantric philosophies of the East, and the Alchemical wisdom of the West. And this is where the two circles of Druidry and Wicca meet and merge – in the alchemical wedding of God and Goddess, in the mystery of Divine Love, and also in the identical aims of Ovate and Witch to heal and to work with the powers of Nature, the powers of star and stone, animal and plant.

It is as if the two founding fathers of modern Wicca and Druidry, Gerald Gardner and Ross Nichols, caught different parts of the mystery as they dipped their hands into the well. Nichols caught the magic of the Bard, the magic of history and the written and spoken word, Gardner caught the magic of God and Goddess, the thrill of the spiral dance and the union of cup and wand.

Combined, their contributions to modern paganism blossom, gaining authenticity and breadth, vitality and depth. Enriched with that sense of continuity and tradition that comes from the Bardic stories, Gardner's Wicca can draw upon myths and images from the land and culture in which it was born. Enriched with an awareness of the inherent sexuality of life within spirituality, Nichols' Druidry is refreshed at its roots.

In the last years of his life, while Nichols worked on *The Book of Druidry*, laying out most of what he had learned about the Druid way, he carved two figures of the God and the Goddess out of two tree trunks. Once they were carved, he painted them in bright colours. He did this outside his hut at the Five Acres Naturist resort, where Gerald Gardner had developed his first coven.

As he carved the wood, allowing the images of Goddess and God to emerge beneath his blade, he must have ruminated on the fact that his friend Gerald had built a new religion based on these two figures and their interaction, while he, Ross, had chosen to act as proponent of another style of Nature Spirituality which stressed not so much the Divine Mother and Father and their interaction, but the fruit of their interaction instead – creativity in all its forms. Unwittingly, they had developed two perfectly complementary systems, which can be combined to create a spiritual path rooted deep in the mythology and soul of these lands.

Each system, like each circle of the Glastonbury well cover is complete in itself. Whoever has truly worked with either knows this. But if allowed to meet, both systems interact to create a third way – a way that we can call, if we wish, Druidcraft.

This way is centred upon a love of life and the natural world, not upon a desire to transcend or escape it. The story from Irish tradition of King Cormac's encounter with the sea-god Manannan mac Lir perfectly describes this type of sensuous spirituality that recognizes the existence of both this world and the Otherworld, and which advocates drawing strength and sustenance from both realms. In the story, Cormac is shown a pool with five streams running from it. Manannan explains to Cormac that those who are wise drink from each of the five streams and from the pool itself, and that each of the streams represents one of the senses, while the pool represents Spirit – the deep centre within each of us.

Inspired by the images and ideas evoked by such tales, and by the worlds of Witch and Druid, we can follow a path today that has been sketched out by writers such as Nichols and Gardner, and those who have followed since. Druidcraft, Druidry and Wicca, are ways of empowerment and of freedom – not dogmatic religious systems, but new spiritualities, magical ones, that draw their inspiration from the ancient past, while offering ways of celebration and working that are constantly changing and evolving. Rather than presenting us with ready-made systems that we must slavishly adopt wholesale, they offer instead inspiration and the ingredients that we can creatively use to fashion our own unique path to suit our own unique lives.

The reason most of us are drawn to such paths, rather than to one of the mainstream ready-made religions offering 'all the answers', is that somewhere inside we understand that we are not supposed to be a passive consumer of spirituality, but instead an active participant in a life that is inherently spiritual. We are not in the restaurant, we are in the kitchen! Earth religions like Druidry and Wicca offer us ingredients — ideas for rituals, stories, folklore, techniques — that can be combined in dozens of different ways to provide us, our family and friends with exactly what we need. They are ways of empowerment, because they put us in charge of our lives, not ways of disempowerment with a priest or guru telling us what to do.

In the end, it all boils down to this. There is you and the ocean, you and the sky, you and the land, now and here. The old lore is not meant to remain preserved in a glass case; it is meant to be used, changed, added to and improved. It only stays alive if each of us takes it and uses it in our own way, with our own creative additions and insights, to help us live a life of depth and meaning, beauty and celebration, here and now — upon this earth, beneath this sky, beside this sea.

> The brilliance of the seas has flashed forth.
> The dawn of blessing has arisen.
> What IS this ancient wisdom?
> The source of these living waters is in your head
> And in your eyes.

> Rumi

RESOURCES

CHAPTER 1

You can see pictures of the well cover and the magical garden in Glastonbury known as the Chalice Well Garden at www.chalicewell.org.uk

Celtic scholar Erynn Laurie, writes: 'In old Irish, the word for a druid was spelled *drui* and druidcraft is *druidecht*. Later it would be spelled *draidecht* or *draoidheachd*. In modern Irish, druid is *draoi*, and Druidcraft is *draoidocht*.'

Gardner and Nichols were both interested in the early British Church and became ordained in obscure unorthodox branches of Christianity: Gardner in the Ancient British Church in 1949, Nichols in the Ancient Celtic Church in 1963.

More details on Nichols and Gardner can be found in *In The Grove of the Druids – The Druid Teachings of Ross Nichols*, edited by Philip Carr-Gomm and on the website http://druidry.org

To explore how the modern version of Wicca was developed by Gerald Gardner, *see* Ronald Hutton, *The Triumph of The Moon*. For a detailed analysis of the sources of Wiccan rituals, *see* Janet and Stewart Farrar, *Witches' Bible*. For further information about how the teachings and rituals were developed, *see* Doreen Valiente, *The Rebirth of Witchcraft*. For details of the many varieties of Wicca that have evolved in modern times, *see* Margot Adler, *Drawing Down the Moon*.

To explore how the modern version of Druidry was developed by Ross Nichols, *see In the Grove of the Druids – The Druid Teachings of Ross Nichols*, edited by Philip Carr-Gomm, and the biography of Ross Nichols on http://druidry.org

To explore the connections between Witchcraft, Druidry and shamanism, *see* Tom Cowan, *Fire in the Head – Shamanism and the Celtic Spirit.*

Regarding the use of the term Witch, Ronald Hutton, Professor of History at Bristol University and expert on the history of Wicca and Witchcraft, says: 'Perhaps most modern Western liberals might think of a witch-doctor, shaman or wizard when they hear the term Witch. But most people, even in their society, would think of a cackling evil old woman – and they would be wholly traditional in doing so. The Anglo-Saxon words "wicce" and "wicca" mean a human who uses magic to harm other humans. By contrast, the wise-folk and cunning-folk were there to use magic to help others, most notably by removing or breaking the spells of the witches. A witch-doctor is not a witch who is a doctor, but a doctor who combats witches, which is what such figures do in tribal societies. The term "white witches" was first applied to wise-folk by seventeenth-century Puritans intent on combating popular magic, as a term of abuse.' [from a letter].

In a complete reversal, the term Witch and Wicca is now used in Pagan and New Age circles to mean someone who uses magic not to harm others but to help and heal them, and someone – in addition – who follows a spiritual path that draws its inspiration from the Natural world. Throughout this book, this modern positive use of the term applies.

For the significance of Avronelle and the Long Man of Wilmington, *see* Philip Carr-Gomm, *The Druid Way*.

CHAPTER 2

The selkie story was adapted from one of the many selkie tales given in David Thomson, *The People of the Sea*. If you wish to explore some of the meaning and depth in the selkie stories, read the chapter 'Seal Skin Soul Skin' in *Women Who Run with the Wolves* by Clarissa Pinkola Estes, and the entry for the Seal in *The Druid Animal Oracle* by Philip and Stephanie Carr-Gomm.

In Gerald Gardner's *Witchcraft Today*, a book produced with considerable help from Ross Nichols, a final note at the end of the book (left out in some later editions) says: 'Diana of Ephesus wore a necklace of acorns; many Celtic goddesses are mentioned as wearing them. At witch meetings every woman must wear one.' You might like to make one for your own dedication ceremony, since the oak is also deeply connected to Druidry. (Not all scholars are able to agree about the etymology of the word 'Druid', but most modern authorities agree with the classical authors that the most likely derivation is from the word for oak, combined with the Indo-European root 'wid' – to know – giving us 'One with knowledge of the oak' or 'Wise person of the oak'.)

If you are interested in comparing the Wiccan and Druid style of circle-casting and calling to the quarters, you can read of the Wiccan style in Vivianne Crowley's *Wicca* and of the Druid style in *Druidry* by Philip Shallcrass. These books also give good surveys of both Wicca and Druidry that you may find them helpful in developing your own unique practice of Druidcraft.

CHAPTER 3

The Bard's tale was developed from 'The Dream of Oengus' in *Early Irish Myths and Sagas*, translated and edited by Jeffrey Gantz. *See also* T.W. Rolleston, *Myths and Legends of the Celtic Race*. The story is the source of inspiration for W.B. Yeats' poem, 'The Dream of Wandering Aengus'.

A reproduction of the Cumbrian altar-stone can be seen in the 'Adder' card of Philip and Stephanie Carr-Gomm's *The Druid Animal Oracle*.

In addition to Nichols citing Jainism in the excerpt quoted in this chapter from *In The Grove of the Druids*, the following excerpt from the introductory booklet that he wrote first for the Ancient Druid Order, and then adapted for the Order of Bards Ovates and Druids, is relevant to the whole theme of this book:

> *The origins of Druidic traditions go back to a past remote indeed, almost as far back as civilisation itself, and at least into Neolithic times. There are links with Aryan and early Hindu culture and what is now the witch cult: reverence for both sun and moon, fivefold and threefold bases of teaching, circular dancing as worship, burning of the dead, the cult of certain animals, the existence of a priest-ruler caste, transmission of teaching by long memorised poems. The Draus or Druis, a cult within the Jain community, have striking similarities to the western Druids (Latin drus: possibly cognate with drau). Amongst them are stone circles around upright stone altars.*

Jainism does have Dravidian roots, and in the past some scholars have seen links between the Dravidians and the Druids, but both the Druidism reported by the Classical authors, and its modern manifestations seem to bear little resemblance to Jainism past or present.

For an historical exploration of love, marriage and sexuality in the Celtic world that looks at Druidic, Witchcraft and Christian influences, *see* Peter Cherici, *Celtic Sexuality – Power, Paradigms and Passions*.

For a discussion on Sacred Sexuality in the Druid Tradition, *see* Maya Sutton and Nicholas Mann, *Druid Magic*.

For an excellent experiential guide to Alchemy and a glimpse into the relationship between the approaches of Sacred Sexuality in East and West through Tantra and Alchemy, *see* Jay Ramsay, *Alchemy – The Art of Transformation*.

For a guide to Sacred Sexuality whose practices can easily be adapted for use within a Druidcraft context, *see* Margot Anand, *The Art of Sexual Ecstasy – The Path of Sacred Sexuality for Western Lovers*.

CHAPTER 4

The Bard's tale was developed from accounts of Brighid in Peter Beresford-Ellis, *The Druids*.

Most introductory books on Wicca and Druidry discuss the seasonal ceremonies, and if you are interested in the history and folklore of the festivals, read *The Stations of the Sun* by Ronald Hutton.

The distance-learning course of The Order of Bards, Ovates and Druids teaches you how to work with the seasonal rites by sending you *The Book of Ritual* that explains how to enact the ceremonies, and the significance of each part of them. Before each festival time you are sent teaching material that gives information on the history, folklore and spiritual significance of the approaching time, and it then offers a solo ritual and a group ritual which you can use or adapt to celebrate in your own way.

CHAPTER 5

The Bard's Tale was developed from an account of the tale in *A Druid's Herbal for the Sacred Earth Year* by Ellen Evert Hopman.

The prayer to the Goddess from the English Herbal is in the British Library – BMs.MS.Harley, 1585 ff12v–13r.

Healing retreats and a distance-learning course in healing within a Druidic context are available through The Druid College of Healing of The Order of Bards, Ovates and Druids. Visualization exercises, Mud baths and sweathouse ceremonies are also held at Druid camps. (*See* http://druidry.org for details.)

Healing Threads – Traditional Medicines of the Highlands and Islands by Mary Beith is an excellent book that offers both a history of early healing practices and a directory of remedies and cures. It is based on research into medieval Gaelic medical manuscripts and the papers of medical societies.

Very little has been published on the use of Celtic sweathouses, but an interesting article that refers to this, and to the healing use of dreams, is 'Auguries, Dreams and Incubatory Sleep' by John Matthews, in *Psychology & the Spiritual Traditions*, R.J. Stewart (ed).

See also Dr Andrew Allen's and Ellen Evert Hopman's books already mentioned, *Anam Cara Spiritual Wisdom from the Celtic World* by John O'Donohue and the section on healing in *The Druid Renaissance* edited by Philip Carr-Gomm.

CHAPTER 6

The Bard's tale was developed from an account in *The Metrical Dindschenchas*, a medieval work that recounts the ancient lore associated with features of the Irish landscape.

The quotation from Charles Mackay's work on Druidic chants comes from 'Druidical Chants Preserved in the Choruses of Popular Songs in England, Scotland, Ireland and France', Charles Mackay, in *The Celtic Magazine*, reproduced in *The Druid Source Book*, John Matthews (ed).

In the section on Questing Magic, divination with totem animals and Ogham is mentioned. Animal and Ogham lore is taught in the Ovate Grade distance-learning course of The Order of Bards, Ovates and Druids, and various oracular systems have been developed – *The Druid Animal Oracle* by Philip and Stephanie Carr-Gomm; an Ogham oracle with cards is available as *The Celtic Tree Oracle* by Liz and Colin Murray, or with wooden Ogham sticks as *Celtic Wisdom Sticks* by Caitlin Matthews.

Most books on Wicca deal with the subject of spells and magic, and a section on Druidic spells can be found in Lewis Spence, *The History and Origins of Druidism*. For examples of many types of spells, see Robin Skelton, *Spellcraft*, and Witch Bree, *Witch's Brew Good Spells for Healing*.

CHAPTER 7

The poem, 'A Human Situation' by Ross Nichols appears in *Prophet Priest and King – The Poetry of Philip Ross Nichols*, edited by Jay Ramsay.

There are now many Druid and Wiccan groups around the world, as any web search will reveal.

For a good guide to Wiccan and other Pagan groups see *The Circle Guide*, available from Circle Sanctuary, PO Box 219, Mt. Horeb, WI 53572 USA, http://www.circlsanctuary.org

For a good guide to Druid groups see *A Druid Directory* by Philip Shallcrass and Emma Restall Orr, available from The British Druid Order, PO Box 1217, Devizes, Wiltshire SN10 4XA, http://druidorder. demon.co.uk. The British Druid Order also publishes books and periodicals and organises workshops and events.

The Order of Bards Ovates and Druids offers a distance-learning programme in Druidry and Druidcraft together with a Sacred Grove planting programme and campaign for Ecological Responsibility. For full details, contact the Order at:

The Order of Bards Ovates and Druids
PO Box 1333
Lewes
East Sussex BN7 1DX
UK

Tel/fax: 44 (0)1273 419129
email: office@druidry.org
Website: http://druidry.org

BIBLIOGRAPHY

Margot Adler, *Drawing Down the Moon*, Beacon Press, 1986

Dr Andrew Allen, *A Dictionary of Sussex Folk Medicine*, Countryside Books, 1995

Margot Anand, *The Art of Sexual Ecstasy – The Path of Sacred Sexuality for Western Lovers*, Thorsons, 1989

Mary Beith, *Healing Threads – Traditional Medicines of the Highlands and Islands*, Polygon, Edinburgh, 1995

Peter Beresford-Ellis, *The Druids*, Eerdmans, 1995

Witch Bree, *Witch's Brew Good Spells for Healing*, Chronicle Books, 2001

Alexander Carmichael, *Carmina Gadelica – Hymns and Incantations*, Floris Books, 1992

Edward Carpenter, *Civilisation, its Cause and Cure*, 1889

Philip Carr-Gomm (ed), *The Druid Renaissance*, Thorsons, 1996

Philip Carr-Gomm, *The Druid Way*, Element Books 1993

Philip Carr-Gomm, *In the Grove of the Druids – The Druid Teachings of Ross Nichols* (ed), Watkins, 2002

Philip and Stephanie Carr-Gomm, *The Druid Animal Oracle*, Fireside Books, USA, 1994; Connections, UK, 1996

Peter Cherici, *Celtic Sexuality – Power, Paradigms and Passions*, Duckworth, 1995

Tom Cowan, *Fire in the Head – Shamanism and the Celtic Spirit*, HarperSanFrancisco, 1993

Vivianne Crowley, *Wicca*, Thorsons, 2000

Clarissa Pinkola Estes, *Women Who Run with the Wolves*, Rider, 2001

Janet and Stewart Farrar, *Witches' Bible*, Robert Hale, 1998

Jeffrey Gantz (trans/ed), *Early Irish Myths and Sagas*, Penguin, 1981

Gerald Gardner, *The Meaning of Witchcraft*, IHO Books, 1999

Gerald Gardner, *Witchcraft Today*, Rider, 1954

E. Gwynn (trans/ed), *The Metrical Dindshenchas,* Dublin 1903-35

Ellen Evert Hopman, *A Druid's Herbal for the Sacred Earth Year*, Destiny Books, 1995

Ronald Hutton, *The Stations of the Sun*, Oxford University Press, 1996

Ronald Hutton, *The Triumph of The Moon*, Oxford University Press, 2000

Caitlin Matthews, *Celtic Wisdom Sticks*, Connections, 2001

John Matthews (ed), *The Druid Source Book*, Blandford, 1996

Marian McNeill (ed), *The Silver Bough*, William MacLellan, 1959

Liz and Colin Murray, *The Celtic Tree Oracle*, Connections, 1996

Ross Nichols, *The Book of Druidry*, Thorsons, 1992

John O'Donohue, *Anam Cara Spiritual Wisdom from the Celtic World*, Bantam, 1999

Jay Ramsay, *Alchemy – The Art of Transformation*, Thorsons, 1997

Jay Ramsay (ed), *Prophet Priest and King – The Poetry of Philip Ross Nichols*, Oak Tree Press, 2001

Emma Restall Orr, *Druidry,* Thorsons, 2001

Emma Restall Orr, *Thorsons Principles of Druidry*, Thorsons, 1998

T.W. Rolleston, *Myths and Legends of the Celtic Race*, Constable, 1985

Philip Shallcrass, *Druidry*, Piatkus, 2000

Robin Skelton, *Spellcraft*, Phoenix, 1978

Lewis Spence, *The History and Origins of Druidism*, Aquarian Press, 1971

R.J. Stewart (ed), *Psychology and the Spiritual Traditions*, Element Books, 1990

Maya Sutton and Nicholas Mann, *Druid Magic*, Llewellyn Books, 2000

David Thomson, *The People of the Sea*, John Day, 1955

Doreen Valiente, *The Rebirth of Witchcraft*, Phoenix, 1989

 INDEX